dedication

To Murray and Ruth Johnson, who encouraged me to pursue my passion

All my customers, past, present and future

Shirley, my wife, partner and ally

Oliver, my son

To whoever said 'Success comes to those who don't go looking for it'

e'cco: here it is ...

écco

contents

écco
licensed bistro
écco

introduction

If I started by telling you that the Great Gorgonzola Theory is the basis for all that I believe and all that I do both in and out of the kitchen, anyone who's not a fan of this challenging – yet rewarding – cheese would probably avert their eyes and speedily turn the page.

So I'll come back to that later.

Why a restaurant? Why e'cco? Why, now, a cookbook?

When I qualified as a chef in 1979, it was my job, no more and no less. That's the way I felt until I went to London and worked at Antony Worrall Thompson's restaurant, Ménage à Trois. It was an original, very exclusive establishment that served only entrees and desserts, no main courses at all. 'Stunned' is the word: I'd never seen anything like the food these chefs were presenting and I realised that the incredible variety of produce available to them was the key.

When I came back to Australia a few years later, our own produce revolution – supply driven by demand – was getting underway. Taking over Le Bronx at New Farm in 1988 was my first outing as owner/chef and these were more discovery years: five stimulating, fascinating, mind-expanding years to explore the theory that good cooking is a matter of doing the simple things well. It was around this time that the idea of a cookbook first floated into my head. And quietly sat there.

In 1994, after brief spells at Café 84 and Continental Café in Brisbane, I went back to London and worked at Antony Worrall Thompson's bistro dell'Ugo.

When my wife, Shirley, and I came home to Brisbane that year, we were ready to open e'cco. How fortunate we were, then, to meet two architects of the calibre of Robert Riddel, now our landlord, and the gifted David Gole – both made invaluable contributions to the style and spirit of e'cco.

e'cco is a bistro by name and a bistro by nature.

A bistro is minimalist at heart, no extravagant flourishes, no pointless additions to a simply-conceived dish. But it's honestly welcoming and glad to see you, whether you're coming in for a salad and a glass of wine, a couple of courses, or making an occasion of it.

Philip Johnson cooks from the heart, with an unparalleled ability to allow ingredients to speak for themselves.

CHERRY RIPE
Food writer and palateer

I've been lucky enough to have several memorable meals at e'cco and I just love Philip's clever approach to flavour. His no-fuss presentation and the simplicity of his dishes are deceptive – Philip is a fabulous cook.

JOAN CAMPBELL
Food Director,
Condé Nast Publications

Philip's recipes have an elegant simplicity about them, which is not surprising. That's what e'cco's like, everything done with stylish restraint. But like e'cco this book tells a story of the joy and delight of fresh food.

RICK STEIN
The Seafood Restaurant, Cornwall, UK

Philip Johnson's book is about my kind of food. These are no nonsense, stylish recipes, that rely on the best and the freshest ingredients. This is what Australian food is all about – I want to cook every recipe.

KATHY SNOWBALL
Food Editor, *Australian Gourmet Traveller*

Bistro food is food that's easy to take, food you can go back to again and again. We have some regular customers who are in two or three times a week.

If you put any classically trained chef into a bistro situation, his or her food is going to show the influence of both. It will have some of the flair and finish of the fine dining style, but be more approachable and less formal. At the same time, it will have more depth and breadth than the bistro staples of steak and chips and coq au vin.

At e'cco, we invest our greatest efforts in showcasing the ingredients, letting flavours speak for themselves. I don't want my food to look like it's been fiddled with and fussed over. I care about quality to the point of obsession but after that, I want to do as little as possible with the very best raw materials.

One of the translations of the Italian word e'cco is 'here is'. That's the essence of what I aim for in any dish. The essential 'here is' element: good food, seasonal food, food that tastes like what it is.

Of course, to get to that point, you've got to work without a net occasionally, be a little daring and give your imagination free rein. You've got to experiment, refine, taste, taste and taste again. And you've got to know when to stop.

Discipline is simplicity is perfection.

That is just as true for people cooking at home as it is in any restaurant.

It was people who love to cook as much as they love to eat that brought the idea of a book percolating to the front of my mind again. So many of our e'cco customers have asked about a recipe, or wondered out loud how we thought of this or that combination, that I thought it was time to share my ideas more widely.

The recipes in this book are true to the spirit of e'cco. They feature familiar and delicious ingredients, requiring consistently good quality if you're going to achieve the most rewarding results.

Many of the soups, first and second courses, side dishes, desserts and ice creams are perennial favourites. They come and go from the e'cco menu according to the seasons. Some, in fact, are so popular with customers that we can't, don't, won't ever do without them. There are other timeless dishes from the Le Bronx days that have been looked up, dusted off and proudly included.

Chockfull of approachable recipes that you can taste as you read them, this excellent book will bring the lapsed cooks rushing back to the stove.

SUE FAIRLIE-CUNINGHAME

Putting this book together, for people who cook at home for the love of it, has been a pleasure. And an effort, digging back into a sometimes unreliable memory. I hope that the result will give you some of the enjoyment it has given all of us at e'cco in writing it.

And the Great Gorgonzola Theory? It's a little story from my earlier years. A dish of gnocchi was on the menu, with gorgonzola among its ingredients. One evening, a lady who'd ordered it was complimenting us on the rest of her meal but said the gorgonzola was too strong, overpowering the gnocchi.

Since discovering e'cco, eating in Brisbane has taken on a new dimension. I feel much empathy with e'cco's food.

MAGGIE BEER
Cook, writer, food producer

After thinking about it overnight, I adapted the dish the next day and cut down the quantity. Another diner who then ordered the gnocchi said how much more he would have enjoyed it – if only there had been more gorgonzola in it.

It made me realise that, if you lose your own vision, you have no point of reference. Find what you like, decide on what you want and stick to it.

Philip Johnson

soups

Sweet potato, chickpea and truffle oil
Potato, leek, smoked salmon and poached egg
White bean, pancetta, tomato and chard
Tomato, roast peppers and pesto
Potato, rocket and goat's cheese
Roast chicken, asparagus, sweet corn and chilli
Spiced lamb and lentil

Sweet potato, chickpea and truffle oil

Serves 10

1 tablespoon unsalted butter
1 tablespoon olive oil
2 medium leeks, sliced and well washed
1 onion, diced
1.5kg (3½ lb) orange sweet potatoes, peeled and roughly chopped
1 large potato, peeled and roughly chopped
2 litres (3½ pt) chicken stock (Basics page 176)
salt/pepper
750g (1 lb 10 oz/3 cups) cooked chickpeas (Basics page 164)
crème fraîche (see Glossary)
truffle oil (see Glossary)

Heat butter and olive oil in a large saucepan over medium heat. Add leeks and onion and sauté until onion is transparent. Add potatoes and cook for 5 minutes.

Add chicken stock, bring to the boil and season well with salt and black pepper. Reduce heat and simmer until vegetables are soft. Add half the cooked chickpeas. Purée mixture, in batches, in a blender until smooth. Return soup to a clean saucepan, add remaining chickpeas and adjust seasonings.

To serve, reheat soup and ladle into bowls. Add a spoonful of crème fraîche, then drizzle with a little truffle oil.

Potato, leek, smoked salmon and poached egg

Serves 6

2 tablespoons olive oil
6 leeks, thinly sliced, well washed
2 onions, diced
3 cloves garlic, finely chopped
10 pink-skinned waxy potatoes such as desiree, peeled and thinly sliced
2 litres (3½ pt) chicken stock (Basics page 176)
salt/pepper
12 slices smoked salmon
6 soft poached eggs (Basics page 165)
⅓ cup chives, chopped

Heat oil in a large saucepan over low heat. Add leeks, onions and garlic and sweat vegetables until onions are transparent. Add potatoes and cook a further 8 minutes. Add chicken stock and bring to the boil, skimming off any impurities that rise to the surface, continue to cook until potatoes are soft. Purée soup, in batches, in a blender until smooth. Return soup to a clean saucepan, season with salt and black pepper and reheat.

To serve, ladle soup into bowls and top with two slices of smoked salmon. Sit a poached egg next to salmon and season with freshly ground black pepper. Scatter chopped chives over egg and salmon.

Chard (silverbeet) is a robustly flavoured leaf also known as swiss chard and should not be confused with the more delicate English spinach. Red chard has bright red stems and is also known as ruby chard or red swiss chard. Always choose young chard for best results.

White bean, pancetta, tomato and chard

Serves 6-8

- 250g (9 oz/1 1/4 cups) dried white beans such as cannellini or navy (haricot)
- 2 tablespoons olive oil
- 400g (13 oz) pancetta in one piece, cut into lardons (see Glossary)
- 2 onions, diced
- 3 sticks celery, diced
- 5 cloves garlic, finely chopped
- 8 roma (italian plum) tomatoes, skinned and diced
- 400g (13 oz) can roma (italian plum) tomatoes
- 750ml (1 1/4 pt) chicken stock (Basics page 176)
- 75g (2 1/2 oz or 1/2 bunch) young swiss chard (silverbeet), stems removed
- 75g (2 1/2 oz or 1/2 bunch) young ruby chard (red swiss chard), stems removed
- salt/pepper
- extra-virgin olive oil
- flat-leaf parsley or basil leaves (chop just prior to serving)
- crusty bread

Cook beans as directed for chickpeas (Basics page 164)

Heat olive oil in a large saucepan over high heat and sauté pancetta until golden. Reduce heat to moderate, add onions, celery and garlic and cook until onions are transparent.

Add fresh and canned tomatoes and chicken stock and bring to the boil, skimming off any impurities that rise to the surface. Add cooked beans, reduce heat and simmer for 20 minutes.

Add well-washed, thickly shredded chard and season with salt and black pepper.

To serve, ladle soup into bowls, drizzle with a little extra-virgin olive oil, scatter with parsley or basil and serve with warm crusty bread.

Tomato, roast peppers and pesto

Serves 6

2 tablespoons olive oil

2 large onions, finely diced

6 cloves garlic, finely chopped

2 teaspoons italian tomato paste (concentrated purée)

18-20 ripe roma (italian plum) tomatoes, skinned and diced

400g (13 oz) can roma (italian plum) tomatoes, sieved

2 teaspoons thyme leaves, chopped

salt/pepper

2 red peppers (capsicum), roasted, peeled and diced (Basics page 164)

600ml (20 fl oz) chicken stock (Basics page 176)

3 tablespoons flat-leaf parsley, finely sliced

pesto (Basics page 166)

ciabatta, or other italian bread, toasted (see Glossary)

Heat olive oil in a large saucepan over moderate heat. Add onions and garlic and sauté until transparent. Add tomato paste and cook, stirring, for 2 minutes. Add fresh and canned tomatoes, bring to the boil and season with thyme, salt and black pepper.

Reduce heat, add peppers and cook for 5 minutes. Pour in enough chicken stock to bring soup to desired consistency. Taste and adjust seasoning, then stir in parsley.

To serve, ladle soup into bowls, top with pesto and serve with toasted bread.

Potato, rocket and goat's cheese

Serves 6

2 tablespoons olive oil

6 leeks, diced and well washed

3 onions, halved and thinly sliced

3 cloves garlic, finely chopped

10 pink-skinned waxy potatoes such as desiree, peeled and thinly sliced

salt/pepper

2 litres (3½ pt) chicken stock (Basics page 176)

120g (4 oz) rocket, stems removed

180g (6 oz) goat's cheese (see Glossary)

Heat oil in a large saucepan over moderate heat. Add leeks, onions and garlic and sweat vegetables for 6-8 minutes or until onion is transparent. Add potatoes, season with salt and black pepper and cook a further 2 minutes.

Add chicken stock and bring to the boil, skimming off any impurities that rise to the surface. Reduce heat and simmer until potatoes are tender. Purée mixture, in batches, in a blender until smooth. Return soup to a clean saucepan and reheat.

To serve, shred the rocket and add to soup, taste and adjust seasonings. Serve soup garnished with crumbled goat's cheese.

This soup is best made 24 hours in advance to allow flavours to develop.

Roast chicken, asparagus, sweet corn and chilli

Serves 6

2 tablespoons olive oil

3 small leeks, sliced into rings and well washed

2 medium brown onions, diced

2 cobs sweet corn, kernels removed

½ head garlic, peeled and sliced

1 red chilli, seeded and thinly sliced (see Glossary)

6 medium pink-skinned waxy potatoes such as desiree, peeled and thinly sliced

1.75 litres (3 pt) roasted chicken stock (Basics page 177)

salt/pepper

1 bunch (220g/8 oz) fresh asparagus, woody ends removed

3 chicken thigh-and-leg portions, roasted

herbs such as chives, chervil or parsley, chopped

Heat olive oil in a large, heavy-based saucepan over moderate heat. Add leeks, onions, corn kernels, garlic and chilli and sweat vegetables until onions are transparent. Add potatoes and cook a further 5 minutes. Add stock and cook until potatoes are tender. Season well with salt and black pepper.

To serve, bring soup to the boil. Cut asparagus diagonally into 2cm (¾ in) lengths. Thickly slice roasted chicken flesh and add to soup with the asparagus. Cook until asparagus is just tender, then fold in herbs and ladle into bowls.

Spiced lamb and lentil

Serves 10

250g (9 oz) french green lentils (du Puy)
80ml (2$^1/_2$ fl oz) olive oil
750g (1 lb 10 oz) diced lamb leg
6 sticks celery, diced
3 onions, diced
4 cloves garlic, finely chopped
$^1/_4$ teaspoon cumin seed, roasted and ground
$^1/_4$ teaspoon coriander seed, roasted and ground
$^1/_4$ teaspoon ground turmeric
$^1/_4$ teaspoon dried chilli flakes
$^1/_4$ teaspoon cracked black pepper
pinch cayenne pepper
pinch saffron threads
2.5 litres (4$^1/_2$ pts) light beef stock, or half chicken and half beef stock (Basics page 176)
8 roma (italian plum) tomatoes, skinned and diced
salt/pepper
250g (9 oz) greek-style natural yoghurt
extra-virgin olive oil
crusty bread

Wash lentils, place in a small saucepan and cover with cold water. Bring to the boil, reduce heat and simmer until lentils are tender, about 15 minutes. Drain and set aside.

Heat oil in a large heavy-based saucepan over moderate heat and brown the lamb, in batches, on all sides. Add celery, onions, garlic and spices, cook, stirring, for 5 minutes. Add stock and bring to the boil, skimming off any impurities that rise to the surface. Reduce heat and simmer until lamb is tender, about 30 minutes, skimming occasionally.

Add cooked lentils and diced tomatoes to the soup and simmer a further 10 minutes. Taste and adjust seasonings.

To serve, ladle soup into bowls and top with a spoonful of yoghurt and a drizzle of extra-virgin olive oil. Serve with crusty bread.

Roast field mushrooms, olive toast, truffle oil, parmesan and rocket (recipe page 36)

starters

Aged goat's cheese, marinated artichokes and tapenade crostini
Baked ricotta cake with mushrooms and roast tomatoes
Porcini mushroom and gorgonzola tart with pear and walnuts
Fresh fig, gorgonzola and prosciutto
Goat's cheese and braised leek pie with bitter greens
Goat's cheese with quince jam, rocket and toasted sourdough
Vine-ripened tomatoes, persian fetta, chilli, basil and garlic bruschetta
Goat's cheese and hazelnut soufflé
Warm jerusalem artichoke pancake, goat's cheese and rocket
Steamed mussels with saffron, chilli, coriander and ginger
Steamed bugs on potato rösti with red pepper essence
Smoked salmon, soft poached egg and chervil vodka cream
Smoked salmon with chilli corncakes, rocket and soused leeks
Seared bugs with skordalia, rocket, ciabatta and sauce vierge
Grilled prawns, tomatoes, chilli, coriander and cornbread
Roast garlic and chicken terrine, cornichons and salsa verde
Seared calf's liver, braised red cabbage and pancetta
Steamed oxtail puddings with shallots and thyme
Buffalo mozzarella with grilled sourdough, warm tomatoes and olives
Roast field mushrooms, olive toast, truffle oil, parmesan and rocket

Left: Fresh fig, gorgonzola and prosciutto (recipe page 17)

Producers such as Gabrielle Kervella from Western Australia and Woodside Cheesewrights in the Adelaide Hills of South Australia are producing some fabulous goat's cheese which, I believe, compare favourably with imported varieties. For this recipe you need to use an unashed, full-flavoured style. Use good quality, bottled Italian artichokes, preferably with stems attached.

Aged goat's cheese, marinated artichokes and tapenade crostini

Serves 6 as a first course

300g (10 oz) aged goat's cheese
125g (4½ oz) fresh ricotta
extra-virgin olive oil
½ cup assorted soft herbs such as chervil, chives, flat-leaf parsley, chopped
freshly ground black pepper

to assemble

tapenade (Basics page 166)
1 french baguette
9 medium marinated artichokes, quartered
chervil sprigs

Combine goat's cheese, ricotta, 1 tablespoon olive oil, chopped herbs and black pepper to taste. Divide mixture into 6 portions. Place an egg ring measuring 7.5 x 1.5cm (3 x ¾ in) on a piece of baking (silicone) paper on a flat surface. Press one portion of the cheese into the ring to shape a flat disc. Repeat with remaining portions, then refrigerate discs, loosely covered, on a flat tray until needed.

Prepare tapenade as recipe directs.

Preheat oven to 180°C (350°F/Gas 4) or a grill to hot. Cut baguette diagonally into twelve slices 5mm (¼ in) thick and about 10cm (4 in) long, drizzle with olive oil and bake or grill on both sides until golden.

To serve, centre a disc of cheese on each serving plate. Arrange artichokes around perimeter of cheese. Spread baguette slices thinly with tapenade and rest against the cheese. Drizzle olive oil over and around the artichokes, garnish with chervil and a good grind of black pepper.

Baked ricotta cake with mushrooms and roast tomatoes

Serves 8 as a first course

clarified butter, melted (Basics page 164)
polenta (yellow cornmeal), for dusting
1kg (2 lb 3 oz) fresh ricotta, semi-firm
4 egg yolks
1/2 cup mixed herbs such as thyme, chives, marjoram, oregano, chopped
1 clove garlic, crushed
1 lemon, finely grated zest only
salt/pepper

to assemble

16 oven-roasted tomato halves (Basics page 165)
extra-virgin olive oil
2 tablespoons unsalted butter
16 large flat or swiss brown mushrooms, wiped
150g (5 oz) rocket, stems removed
truffle oil (see Glossary)

Preheat oven to 160°C (350°F/Gas 3). Line the base of an 18cm (7in) round springform tin with baking (silicone) paper, brush sides of tin with clarified butter and dust with polenta, shaking out the excess.

Place ricotta and egg yolks in a food processor and process to combine. Fold in herbs, garlic, lemon zest and season with salt and black pepper. Spoon mixture into prepared tin, smooth the top using the back of a large metal spoon dipped in hot water. Brush with a little clarified butter and dust with polenta. Bake until cheese is set, 35 to 40 minutes. Remove from oven and allow cake to cool in the tin.

Prepare the oven-roasted tomatoes as recipe directs. Preheat oven to 200°C (400°F/Gas 6). For the mushrooms, heat a large, heavy-based, ovenproof frying pan over high heat. Add a little olive oil and the butter, then add the mushrooms and toss lightly, seasoning to taste with salt and black pepper. Place pan in the oven and roast until mushrooms are tender but not too soft.

To serve, cut ricotta cake into wedges and reheat under a hot grill or in a 180°C (350°F/Gas 4) oven. Stand a wedge on each serving plate and arrange the mushrooms to one side. Add two warmed tomato halves and some rocket. Drizzle a little truffle oil over and around ricotta cake and mushrooms. Season with black pepper.

The inspiration for this tart began as a variation on a stilton and walnut tart I'd seen in London. This dish has proved to be one of our most popular with the recipe often requested. If fresh porcini are unavailable, use good quality canned rather than reconstituted dried porcini, as their texture is too firm. If using canned porcini, drain, slice and sauté as for the fresh porcini. I recommend the imported Italian gorgonzola. At e'cco, we use the Mauri piccante, which is a fully matured style. Corella pears are small and crisp with a striking red/gold skin. In this salad, they are better when crisp rather than too ripe.

Porcini mushroom and gorgonzola tart with pear and walnuts

Serves 8 as a first course

One 24cm (9½ in) blind-baked, savoury shortcrust tart shell (Basics page 174)
6 eggs
600ml (21 fl oz) cream
salt/pepper
400g (13 oz) fresh porcini mushrooms, wiped
extra-virgin olive oil
½ teaspoon crushed garlic
½ cup flat-leaf parsley, shredded
250g (9 oz) italian gorgonzola, fully matured

to assemble

red wine vinaigrette (Basics page 171)
3 corella pears, quartered and sliced
150g (5 oz) watercress or rocket, stems removed
1 small red onion, thinly sliced into rings
90g (3 oz) walnuts (preferably californian), roasted

Prepare tart shell as recipe directs.

Preheat oven to 120°C (250°F/Gas 1/2). Whisk together eggs and cream and season to taste with salt and black pepper. Allow mixture to sit while preparing the filling.

Slice the mushrooms. Heat a little oil in a heavy-based pan over high heat and sauté mushrooms with garlic, salt and black pepper to taste. Remove from heat and stir in the parsley. Spoon mixture evenly into prepared pastry shell, then crumble gorgonzola evenly over the top. Skim the froth from the surface of the custard and pour into pastry shell over the filling. Bake until filling is just set, about 1 hour.

Prepare the vinaigrette as recipe directs. Combine sliced pears, salad leaves, onion and roasted walnuts in a large bowl. Lightly dress with the vinaigrette.

To serve, place a wedge of the warm tart in the centre of each serving plate and arrange a portion of the salad alongside.

See photograph page 30

Another very simple dish relying on several key ingredients that combine well. This dish made the front cover of Australian Gourmet Traveller *magazine. It just goes to show that simplicity can be an art form!*

Fresh fig, gorgonzola and prosciutto

Serves 6 as a first course

6 ripe figs, halved
1 cup basil leaves
300g (10 oz) italian gorgonzola, fully matured
12 thick slices ciabatta, toasted (see Glossary)
18 slices prosciutto, sliced very thinly
extra-virgin olive oil
freshly ground black pepper

To serve, place two fig halves on each plate. Tear the basil leaves and scatter them over the figs. Place a spoonful of gorgonzola and a slice of ciabatta to one side. Drape three prosciutto slices between figs and gorgonzola. Drizzle with extra-virgin olive oil and season with black pepper.

See photograph page 12

Goat's cheese and braised leek pie with bitter greens

Serves 8-10 as a first course

olive oil pastry

300g (10 oz) plain flour
pinch of salt
1 egg
¼ cup (60ml/2 fl oz) olive oil
½ cup (125ml/4½ fl oz) water
1 egg, beaten lightly, for egg wash

cheese and leek filling

75g (2½ oz) unsalted butter
2 medium leeks, sliced and well washed
1 onion, sliced
300g (10 oz) goat's cheese
100g (3½ oz) fetta
½ cup mixed mint and dill, chopped
3 egg yolks
salt/pepper

to assemble

100ml (3½ fl oz) balsamic dressing (Basics page 171)
375g (13 oz) assorted salad leaves such as radicchio, rocket and frisse (young curly endive)
¼ cup mixed flat-leaf parsley and basil leaves
1 small red onion, thinly sliced

For the pastry, place flour and salt in a food processor, add egg and olive oil and process to a crumbly texture. With machine running, add water and process until pastry begins to come together on the blade, do not overwork. Remove from processor and knead lightly.

Place a 24 x 4cm (9½ x 1¾ in) pastry ring on a baking (silicone) paper-lined flat oven tray (or use a fluted deep tart tin with a removable base). Roll out two-thirds of the pastry to about 3mm (⅛ in) thickness and use to line the ring, allowing pastry to overhang sides by 2cm (¾ in). Roll out remaining pastry to make a lid and rest both sections in the refrigerator for 1 hour.

Preheat oven to 180°C (350°F/Gas 4). For the filling, melt butter in a heavy-based pan over low heat. Add leeks and onion and gently sweat until onion is transparent. Remove from heat and cool slightly. Stir in crumbled goat's cheese, fetta, herbs, egg yolks and season well with salt and black pepper.

Fill rested tart shell with the cheese mixture. Place pastry lid on top and lightly brush lid with the egg wash. Fold the pastry overhang back over top towards the centre and egg wash the overhang. Prick lid in the centre a little to allow steam to escape during cooking and bake until pastry is golden, about 40 minutes. Remove pie from oven and allow to cool for 20 minutes before serving.

Prepare balsamic dressing as recipe directs. Wash and spin-dry salad leaves and herbs and place in a bowl. Add onion and toss with enough of the dressing to lightly coat.

To serve, place a wedge of the warm pie on each plate and arrange salad alongside.

We use Maggie Beer's quince paste because it's a great product. Quinces are seasonal and the paste, which has the consistency of thick jam, is time-consuming to prepare, so I'd suggest you do the same. This dish also works well using Italian-style mustard fruits in lieu of quince paste.

Goat's cheese with quince jam, rocket and toasted sourdough

Serves 6 as a first course

- balsamic dressing (Basics page 171)
- 150g (5 oz) rocket, stems removed
- 12 slices sourdough bread, thickly sliced
- extra-virgin olive oil
- 300g (10 oz) mature goat's cheese, white or ashed
- 6 tablespoons quince jam
- freshly ground black pepper

Prepare balsamic dressing as recipe directs. Place rocket in a large bowl and toss lightly with some of the dressing. Drizzle sourdough with olive oil and grill until golden. Place a wedge of goat's cheese on each plate with the salad alongside. Add a spoonful of quince jam and a slice of sourdough, then grind black pepper over the cheese.

Persian Fetta is produced in Victoria's Yarra Valley and sold packed, marinated in olive oil, thyme and garlic. It's quite a soft fetta with a creamy texture.

Vine-ripened tomatoes, persian fetta, chilli, basil and garlic bruschetta

Serves 6 as a first course

- 1 head roasted garlic confit (Basics page 167)
- 300g (10 oz) persian fetta, drained (or best available marinated fetta)
- 6 vine-ripened tomatoes
- 12 slices ciabatta (see Glossary)
- 1 red onion, finely diced
- 1 cup basil leaves
- chilli oil (Basics page 168)
- 6 lemon wedges

Squeeze flesh from garlic confit into a small bowl. In separate bowl beat fetta to soften, adding a little of its marinating oil if necessary. Remove cores from tomatoes, cut each tomato into six slices horizontally. Lay slices to form a circle on each serving plate.

Toast ciabatta then spread with garlic paste. Meanwhile, scatter diced onion and torn basil leaves over tomatoes. Drizzle with chilli oil. Place a spoonful of fetta in the centre of each tomato circle. Add a wedge of lemon and two slices of ciabatta to one side.

Goat's cheese and hazelnut soufflé

Serves 6 as a first course

2 tablespoons unsalted butter, melted
½ cup (75g/2½ oz) polenta (yellow cornmeal)
50g (2 oz) unsalted butter
50g (2 oz) plain flour
300ml (11 fl oz) cream
300ml (11 fl oz) milk
4 sprigs thyme, leaves chopped
pinch nutmeg, freshly grated
salt/pepper
4 egg yolks
225g (8 oz) mature goat's cheese, crumbled
6 egg whites
½ cup (50g /1½ oz) hazelnuts, roasted and finely chopped

Preheat oven to 220°C (425°F/Gas 7). Brush six 180ml (6 fl oz) capacity ceramic soufflé dishes with the melted butter and coat with polenta, shaking out the excess.

Melt the 50g butter in a heavy-based pan over moderate heat, then stir in flour. Cook and stir until mixture begins to leave the sides of the pan, then remove pan from heat. Gradually whisk in cream, then milk until smooth.

Bring mixture to the boil, stirring constantly, cook for a further 5 minutes stirring occasionally. Remove from heat and season with thyme, nutmeg, salt and black pepper to taste. Whisk in egg yolks and goat's cheese, cool slightly. Whisk egg whites until they hold medium peaks and, using a metal spoon, fold into soufflé mixture.

Divide mixture between soufflé dishes and scatter the tops with hazelnuts. Place dishes on an oven tray and bake until soufflés are well risen and golden, about 15-20 minutes. Serve immediately with a green salad.

When Air New Zealand executives tried this dish at e'cco, they were very keen to include it on our first menu for their Pacific flights. They were taken with the simplicity and well-defined flavours. If a blini pan is unavailable, cook the pancakes in an oiled heavy-based frying pan or crêpe pan, turning them over to cook on both sides. If jerusalem artichokes are out of season, make the pancake mix using 750g (1½ lb) potatoes.

Warm jerusalem artichoke pancake, goat's cheese and rocket

Serves 10 as a first course

375g (13 oz) pink-skinned, waxy potatoes such as desiree, peeled and diced
375g (13 oz) jerusalem artichokes, peeled and diced
75g (2½ oz) plain flour
75ml (2½ fl oz) cream
4 eggs, separated
1 tablespoon dijon mustard
salt/pepper
olive oil, for cooking

to assemble

lemon dressing (Basics page 172)
300g (10 oz) rocket, stems removed
1 red onion, thinly sliced
3 jerusalem artichokes, peeled and shaved
¼ cup chives, chopped
500g (17 oz) log fresh goat's cheese
extra-virgin olive oil
wedges of lemon

Boil potatoes and artichokes separately as they cook at different rates, until soft. Drain, return vegetables to saucepan and return to heat for a short time to dry completely. Pass through a mouli or carefully mash. Mix in flour, cream, egg yolks and mustard, season with salt and black pepper. Whisk egg whites until stiff then fold through the mash.

Preheat grill to moderate. Place a blini pan (or a heavy-based frying pan) over moderate heat and brush with olive oil. Fill blini pans with batter (or spoon batter into frying pan in 12cm (5 in) rounds) and cook until coloured on the underside. Place blini pan under the hot grill to firm the tops (or turn pancakes in frying pan and cook the other side). Remove pancakes to a wire rack to cool.

Prepare lemon dressing as recipe directs. Combine rocket, onion, artichokes and chives in a large bowl and toss to coat lightly with some of the dressing.

To serve, centre a pancake on each serving plate. Arrange salad on pancake and top with a thick slice of goat's cheese. Grind black pepper over, drizzle with a little extra-virgin olive oil and add a wedge of lemon.

This e'cco classic was inspired by a similar dish from my time at dell 'Ugo. Fresh mussels should be tightly closed, or should close when tapped. Don't cook any mussel that won't close. Avoid cooking more than two portions together as more than this will drop the heat considerably, inhibiting some of the mussels from opening.

Steamed mussels with saffron, chilli, coriander and ginger

Serves 1 as a first course

pinch of saffron threads
2 teaspoons thai fish sauce
1/2 cup (125ml/4 1/2 fl oz) white wine
1 tablespoon peanut oil
12 fresh black mussels, cleaned and beards removed
1 large knob fresh ginger, peeled and shredded
1 red chilli, sliced into fine rings
1 slice ciabatta (see Glossary)
extra-virgin olive oil
1/4 cup coriander leaves
1/2 lime

Combine saffron, fish sauce and wine and allow to infuse for a minimum of 2 hours.

Heat a heavy-based saucepan (large enough to hold mussels comfortably) over high heat. The pan should be hot enough to sizzle the ginger and boil the saffron mix on contact. Add peanut oil, then the mussels. Stir through ginger and chilli, cover and cook for 30-60 seconds. Keeping heat high, add saffron mixture, cover and cook a further 2-3 minutes or until mussels open. Discard any mussels which do not open.

Meanwhile, drizzle bread with a little extra-virgin olive oil and grill both sides.

To serve, spoon mussels into a bowl, scatter fresh coriander on top and pour pan juices over. Garnish with lime and serve with grilled ciabatta.

Steamed bugs on potato rösti with red pepper essence

Serves 6 as a first course

potato rösti

10 large pink-skinned waxy potatoes such as desiree, peeled
salt/pepper
clarified butter (Basics page 164)

to assemble

red pepper essence (Basics page 172)
hollandaise (Basics page 168)

2 shallots (french shallots), sliced
2 cloves garlic, finely chopped
750g (1 lb 10 oz) moreton bay or balmain bug meat (or use lobster or prawns)
unsalted butter, melted

To make the rösti, grate the potatoes but do not rinse. Squeeze out as much moisture as possible and place in a bowl. Season well with salt and black pepper.

Heat a blini pan (or use greased egg rings in a heavy-based frying pan) over moderate heat and brush with clarified butter. Fill blini pans or shape potato mixture into rounds about 12cm (5 in) in diameter and 2cm (3/4 in) thick and cook until golden on one side. Turn and cook the second side.

Prepare red pepper essence and hollandaise as recipes direct.

Butter six 8cm (3 in) squares of aluminium foil and top each with some shallots, garlic and bug meat. Drizzle a little melted butter over and season with salt and black pepper. Place foil squares into a wide steamer in a single layer. Cover with lid and steam for 6-8 minutes or until flesh is opaque. If a wide steamer is unavailable, use a rack over water in a wok and seal with a lid.

To serve, preheat oven to 180°C (350°F/Gas 4) and reheat the rösti in a single layer on an oven tray. Arrange rösti in the centre of each plate. Using a spatula, remove bugs from each square of foil and place on rösti. Surround with red pepper essence and finish with a spoonful of hollandaise on top of the bugs.

Smoked salmon, soft poached egg and chervil vodka cream

Serves 6 as a first course

6 soft poached eggs (Basics page 165)
12 large slices smoked salmon
30g (1 oz) salmon roe
chervil

chive oil

2 cups chives
250ml (9 fl oz) extra-virgin olive oil

chervil vodka cream

3 egg yolks
1 lime, juice only
1 clove garlic
2 small pickled onions
1 teaspoon salted capers, well rinsed
1 cup (250ml/9 fl oz) extra-virgin olive oil
½ granny smith apple, cored and diced
1 cup chervil
½ cup chives
¼ cup flat-leaf parsley
200ml (7 fl oz) sour cream
2-3 tablespoons vodka
salt/pepper

To make the chive oil, combine chives and oil in a blender (vitamiser – not a food processor). Then pour into a very fine sieve and allow to drain through. Store chive oil in the refrigerator.

To make the chervil cream, place egg yolks, lime juice and garlic in a blender and liquidise. Add pickled onions and capers. With machine running, slowly drizzle in the olive oil until mixture is the consistency of mayonnaise. Continue blending, adding the apple and herbs until mixture is smooth. Transfer mixture to a bowl and lightly whisk in the sour cream and vodka to taste. Strain through a fine sieve. Season with salt and black pepper.

Prepare soft poached eggs as recipe directs. Meanwhile, lay 2 slices of salmon on a board, slightly overlapping, to form a square. Repeat with remaining salmon to make six squares. Centre each cooked, drained egg on a salmon square and fold edges over to totally enclose egg.

To serve, invert each salmon parcel onto the centre of a serving plate. Pour about 60ml (2 fl oz) chervil cream around each parcel, then garnish with a drizzle of chive oil, some salmon roe and chervil leaves. Serve immediately.

Smoked salmon with chilli corncakes, rocket and soused leeks

Serves 4 as a first course

chilli corncakes (Side Dishes page 120)
8 slices smoked salmon, to serve

soused leeks

2 tablespoons unsalted butter
2 leeks, sliced and well washed
1 cup (250ml/9 fl oz) crème fraîche (see Glossary)
1 lemon, grated zest and juice
salt/pepper

rocket salad

100ml (3½ fl oz)
lemon dressing (Basics page 172)
1 tablespoon chives, finely chopped
1 teaspoon coriander seed, roasted and crushed
60g (2 oz) rocket, stems removed
8 oven-roasted tomato halves (Basics page 165)
1 red onion, thinly sliced

Prepare chilli corncakes.

To cook leeks, heat butter in a heavy-based pan over moderate heat until bubbling. Add leeks and sauté until wilted and transparent. Cool leeks completely. Stir in crème fraîche, lemon zest and juice, then season with salt and black pepper.

For the salad, prepare lemon dressing as recipe directs. Combine lemon dressing with chives and crushed coriander seed just prior to serving. Place rocket in a bowl with just enough dressing to moisten, then toss with oven-roasted tomatoes and onion.

To serve, preheat oven to 180°C (350°F/Gas 4). Place corncakes in a single layer on a baking (silicone) paper-lined baking tray and heat in oven until warmed through. Centre a warm corncake on each plate. Top with a spoonful of the soused leeks. Drape with a slice of salmon. Arrange salad on top, then drape with another slice of salmon and drizzle with a little of the dressing. Finish with a grind of black pepper and serve immediately.

I believe it is imperative to always use freshly peeled garlic. Commercial brands generally use additives such as salt, vinegar or sugar as a preservative that drastically taints the fresh flavour of the garlic. The heads of fresh garlic should be young and firm, without any green shoots in the centre of each clove, which can be bitter if not removed.

Seared bugs with skordalia, rocket, ciabatta and sauce vierge

Serves 6 as a first course

olive oil

600g (1 lb 5 oz) moreton bay or balmain bug meat (or use lobster or prawns)

knob of unsalted butter

6 thick slices ciabatta (see Glossary)

120g (4 oz) rocket

skordalia

500g (17 oz) pink-skinned waxy potatoes such as desiree, cooked

1½ tablespoons lemon juice

¼ cup (60ml/2 fl oz) extra-virgin olive oil

2 cloves garlic, finely chopped

salt/pepper

sauce vierge

100ml (3½ fl oz) olive oil

30ml (1 fl oz) lemon juice

1 teaspoon coriander seed, roasted and crushed

freshly ground black pepper

8 basil leaves

2 roma (italian plum) tomatoes, skinned, seeded and diced

To make skordalia, put potatoes through a mouli or mash carefully. Whisk in the lemon juice, olive oil and garlic, taking care not to make the potatoes starchy. Season well with salt and white pepper.

For the sauce vierge, whisk together olive oil, lemon juice and crushed coriander, season well with salt and black pepper. Just prior to serving, shred the basil leaves and stir into sauce with the diced tomato.

Heat a heavy-based pan over high heat and add a little olive oil. Add bug meat and quickly sear until opaque, adding a knob of butter towards the end of cooking time. Meanwhile, toast the ciabatta.

To serve, place a large spoonful of skordalia on each serving plate. Arrange bug meat, rocket and toasted bread alongside, then drizzle sauce over and around bugs.

At e'cco, we have always served this dish hot but when Air New Zealand chose it for their menu they very successfully served it as a chilled starter with toasted cornbread. Cornbread or polenta bread should be available from any traditional bakery. Carol Field's book The Italian Baker *has a recipe both for cornbread and ciabatta. Another good book for Italian breads is* The Il Fornaio Baking Book *by Franco Galli.*

Grilled prawns, tomatoes, chilli, coriander and cornbread

Serves 6 as a first course

2 cups (500mls/18 fl oz) rich tomato sauce (Basics page 171)
36 green (uncooked) medium prawns
2 tablespoons peanut oil
1 tablespoon unsalted butter
2 shallots (french shallots), sliced
2 cloves garlic, crushed
2 red chillies, seeded and thinly sliced
salt/pepper
1 cup coriander leaves
extra-virgin olive oil
lemon wedges
cornbread, sliced and toasted or warmed

Prepare rich tomato sauce as recipe directs.

Shell and devein prawns, leaving tails intact. Heat oil in a heavy-based pan over moderately-high heat, add prawns and sauté on both sides. Add butter, shallots, garlic and chillies. Season with salt and black pepper. Increase heat and toss prawns until cooked – they will become pink and opaque. Remove prawns from pan and reserve.

Add rich tomato sauce to pan, heat through, then return prawns along with any juices. To serve, spoon into wide bowls, scatter with coriander leaves, drizzle with extra-virgin olive oil and finish with a grind of black pepper. Garnish with a lemon wedge and cornbread to one side.

Over the past few years I've worked very closely with friend and chef Peter MacMillan. This recipe is one of his. It has a very simple ingredient list, so the quality of the chicken is paramount. Using a free-range, organic or cornfed chicken makes a huge difference both in flavour and setting quality. Barossa chooks are farmed in South Australia's Barossa Valley by Saskia Beer. Throughout this book we specify good quality sea salt. I recommend only using Maldon sea salt flakes in this recipe. This dish needs to be cooked 24 hours in advance to allow the natural gelatine to set the terrine.

Roast garlic and chicken terrine, cornichons and salsa verde

Serves 10 as a first course

2 x 1.5-1.75kg (3 1/2-4 lb) chickens, or 1 x 3kg (6 lb 10 oz) Barossa chook

2 heads garlic confit (Basics page 167 either method)

1 cup basil leaves

2 teaspoons thyme leaves, chopped

I lemon, grated zest only

salt/pepper

to serve

balsamic dressing (Basics page 171)
mixed salad leaves
cornichons (see Glossary)
crusty bread such as ciabatta (see Glossary)
salsa verde (Basics page 168)

Carefully remove the skin from chicken in one piece if possible and use it to line a terrine mould (see Glossary).

Dice the leg and breast meat into 1-2cm (1/2-3/4 in) pieces and place in a bowl. Add the squeezed flesh from garlic confit, basil, thyme and lemon zest, mix well. Weigh the mixture and, for each 1 kg (2 lb 3oz) of terrine mix, add 1 percent salt and a good grinding of black pepper, i.e if mixture weighs 1.5kg (3 1/2 lb), use 15g (1/2 oz) salt.

Preheat oven to 180°C (350°F/Gas 4). Pack mixture into lined terrine and fold the skin over to enclose the filling. Cover terrine with aluminium foil and place in an ovenproof dish. Fill dish with enough hot water to come halfway up the sides of the terrine and bake for 1 hour.

To check if terrine is cooked through, the internal temperature must be 70°C (158°F). If you do not have a meat thermometer, insert a metal skewer into the centre, wait a short time, remove and feel the temperature of the skewer – it must be quite hot to the touch. Remove terrine from water bath and allow to cool. Refrigerate overnight, placing a weight on the terrine as it cools.

Prepare balsamic dressing as recipe directs and use enough to moisten the salad leaves. Remove the terrine from the mould and cut into 1.5cm (5/8 in) thick slices.

To serve, lay a slice of terrine on each serving plate. Put a small pile of sea salt flakes and freshly ground black pepper on one side with a few cornichons. Place salad on the opposite side with a slice of crusty bread. Drizzle a little of the dressing around the perimeter of the plate. Add a spoonful of salsa verde.

Right: Roast garlic and chicken terrine, cornichons and salsa verde (recipe this page)

Top: Porcini mushroom and gorgonzola tart with pear and walnuts (recipe page 16)

Above: Seared scallops with wakame, coriander, cucumber and lime (recipe page 42)

Right: Seared cuttlefish with cucumber, tomato, roast peppers and chilli oil (recipe page 40)

écco

If preferred, this dish works well with either the champ or parsnip mash (Side Dishes pages 120 and 121).

Seared calf's liver, braised red cabbage and pancetta

Serves 6 as a first course

jus (Basics page 175)

red cabbage with bacon and hazelnuts (Side Dishes page 124)

12 slices pancetta

1kg (2 lb 3 oz) calf's liver

olive oil

3/4 cup flat-leaf parsley, shredded

Prepare jus, and red cabbage with bacon and hazelnuts (omitting bacon) as recipes direct. Crisp the pancetta by sautéeing in a frying pan or grilling then drain on absorbent paper.

Prepare liver by removing skin and sinews and slice thinly, allowing three slices per serving. Heat a little olive oil in a heavy-based shallow pan over very high heat. Add liver and quickly sear, turning once – inside should be still pink.

To serve, centre a mound of warm cabbage on each plate. Rest three slices of liver on top, drizzle hot jus over and around the liver and top with pancetta. Scatter with parsley and serve immediately.

Salad of spinach, pear, gorgonzola, walnuts and crisp bacon (recipe page 38)

You can braise the oxtail one or two days in advance. On the day required, the puddings can be filled and refrigerated ahead of time and steamed just prior to serving. Tandaco suet mix contains 40 percent rendered beef fat and 60 percent flour. If Tandaco brand is unavailable, use a similar product.

Steamed oxtail puddings with shallots and thyme

Serves 6 as a first course

braised oxtail (Basics page 178)
olive oil
1 onion, diced
1 carrot, diced
1 stick celery, diced
1 leek, sliced lengthwise, diced and well washed
1 teaspoon garlic, finely chopped
2 teaspoons thyme leaves, chopped
salt/pepper

suet pastry

250g (9 oz) packet Tandaco suet mix
2 cups (250g/9 oz) plain flour
2 teaspoons baking powder
pinch of salt
250ml (9 fl oz) cold water
1 egg, beaten lightly, for egg wash

30 small shallots (french shallots), unpeeled
1/2 cup flat-leaf parsley, finely chopped

Prepare braised oxtail as recipe directs.

Heat a little oil in a heavy-based pan and sauté the diced vegetables with garlic and thyme until onion is transparent. Fold mixture through the oxtail meat, adding enough of the reduced sauce to moisten, season with salt and pepper.

To make the pastry, place suet mix, flour, baking powder and salt in a food processor and, using the pulse button, process lightly, adding the water to bring pastry together. Knead lightly, wrap in plastic food wrap and rest in refrigerator for one hour.

Roll out pastry very thinly on a floured surface and cut out six circles about 13cm (5 in) in diameter. Grease six 125ml (4 fl oz) metal dariole moulds and line with pastry circles. Roll out remaining pastry and cut lids large enough to overlap the moulds' edges.

Fill moulds with oxtail mixture. Brush egg wash over pastry lids, invert over moulds and press edges together to seal. Trim off excess pastry. Cover moulds with buttered aluminium foil, pressing down snugly.

Steam moulds in a steamer or by sitting moulds on a rack inside a wok and covering with a lid for approximately 30 minutes.

Meanwhile, for the garnish, toss shallots with a little olive oil and roast in a 200°C (400°F/Gas 6) oven until cooked through. Allow to cool, then peel off skins.

To serve, add shallots to the reduced sauce and reheat. Unmould the puddings onto serving plates. Fold parsley into sauce and spoon sauce and shallots over. If desired, accompany with radicchio and bacon (Side Dishes page 127) or wilted spinach.

For many years we have had to be content with cow's milk mozzarella, but with Australia's burgeoning cheese industry, we now have available fresh, traditionally made buffalo milk mozzarella.

Buffalo mozzarella with grilled sourdough, warm tomatoes and olives

Serves 6 as a first course

6 thick slices sourdough bread
1 tablespoon unsalted butter
6 vine-ripened tomatoes, halved
1 cup (150g/5 oz) ligurian olives (see Glossary)
700g (1½ lb) buffalo mozzarella, thickly sliced
½ cup (125g/4½ oz) pesto (Basics page 166)
extra-virgin olive oil

Preheat grill to hot. Grill the sourdough until toasted on both sides.

Melt butter in a heavy-based pan over high heat and sear the tomatoes on both sides. Reduce heat, add the olives and allow them to warm through.

Arrange the mozzarella slices on the toasted bread and place under the grill until cheese begins to melt.

To serve, place one piece of sourdough on each plate with two tomato halves to one side. Spoon olives next to the tomatoes. Top tomatoes with a teaspoon of pesto, then thin some extra pesto with a little olive oil and drizzle around the plate.

Roast field mushrooms, olive toast, truffle oil, parmesan and rocket

Serves 4 as a first course

tapenade (Basics page 166)
balsamic dressing (Basics page 171)
2 tablespoons olive oil
20 x 6-8cm diameter (2½-3¼ in) field mushrooms (swiss browns or open flats), wiped
salt/pepper
knob of unsalted butter
4 slices sourdough bread, toasted
truffle oil (see Glossary)
shaved parmesan
60g (2 oz) rocket, stems removed
1 lemon, quartered

Prepare tapenade and balsamic dressing as recipes direct.

Preheat oven to 220°C (425°F/Gas 7). Heat olive oil in a heavy-based ovenproof pan over moderate heat, add mushrooms, toss, then season with salt and black pepper. Add butter, then place pan in oven and cook for 5-8 minutes or until mushrooms are tender. Drain mushrooms on kitchen paper.

To serve, spread toasted sourdough lightly with tapenade and centre each on a serving plate. Top each toast with five mushrooms and drizzle with truffle oil. Add several slices of shaved parmesan. Toss rocket with enough of the balsamic dressing to moisten lightly and place on parmesan. Garnish each with a lemon wedge and grinding of black pepper.

salads

Salad of spinach, pear, gorgonzola, walnuts and crisp bacon
Salad of baby cos, pear, shaved fennel, pecans and currants
Salad of bugs, pine nuts, red onion, southern golds and watercress
Seared cuttlefish with cucumber, tomato, roast peppers and chilli oil
Rice wine marinated scallops, spiced avocado and gazpacho
Seared scallops with wakame, coriander, cucumber and lime
Grilled quail with crisp pear and green peppercorn dressing
Salad of veal shank, roast garlic, beetroot and red wine vinegar
Salad of cornfed chicken, roast peppers and swiss chard
Salad of slow-cooked duck, spinach, apple and hazelnuts
Salad of chorizo, warm southern golds, peppers and soft poached egg
Grilled quail, witlof, watercress, orange and pecans

Salad of spinach, pear, gorgonzola, walnuts and crisp bacon

Serves 6 as a first course

red wine vinaigrette (Basics page 171)
18 middle eye bacon rashers, very thinly sliced
3 pears, just under-ripe
350g (12 oz) english spinach leaves, stems removed
1 small red onion, very thinly sliced into rings
1 cup (100g/3½ oz) walnuts (preferably californian), roasted
250g (9 oz) italian gorgonzola, fully matured

Prepare red wine vinaigrette as recipe directs. Grill bacon until crisp and drain on absorbent paper.

Quarter and core the pears, then cut each quarter into 3 wedges. Place in a large bowl and add the spinach, onion rings, walnuts, roughly chopped gorgonzola and bacon. Lightly dress with some of the vinaigrette – avoid overmixing. Divide between serving bowls.

See photograph page 32

Salad of baby cos, pear, shaved fennel, pecans and currants

Serves 4 as a first course

½ cup (75g/2½ oz) dried currants
½ cup (125ml/4½ fl oz) red wine vinegar (see Glossary)
extra-virgin olive oil
2 heads baby cos lettuce, leaves separated
1 pear, quartered, cored and thinly sliced
1 small fennel bulb, thinly sliced
1 cup (100g/3½ oz) pecans, roasted and chopped
100g (3½ oz) shaved parmesan
salt/pepper

Place currants and vinegar in a bowl, add 1 tablespoon olive oil and allow to infuse several hours – or overnight, if possible.

In a large bowl, combine cos, pear, fennel, pecans and shaved parmesan. Add drained currants and enough of the vinegar and additional olive oil to moisten. Season well with salt and black pepper. Toss salad to distribute ingredients evenly and coat with dressing.

To serve, divide salad between wide serving bowls, taking care parmesan is well distributed as it tends to clump together.

This has been one of our most popular salads. The combination of warm potatoes with fresh seafood lightened with salad greens makes this a great lunch dish.

Salad of bugs, pine nuts, red onion, southern golds and watercress

Serves 6 as a first course

lemon dressing (Basics page 172)

$\frac{1}{2}$ cup (125ml/4$\frac{1}{2}$ fl oz) roasted garlic mayonnaise (Basics page 167)

18 medium southern gold (pink-eye) potatoes, steamed and peeled

olive oil, for cooking

24 moreton bay or balmain bug tails (or use lobster medallions), shelled

100g (3$\frac{1}{2}$ oz) watercress

100g (3$\frac{1}{2}$ oz) rocket, stems removed

$\frac{1}{2}$ cup (75g/ 2$\frac{1}{2}$ oz) pine nuts, roasted

1 red onion, thinly sliced

$\frac{1}{2}$ cup chives, finely chopped

extra-virgin olive oil

freshly ground black pepper

lemon wedges

Prepare lemon dressing and roasted garlic mayonnaise as recipes direct.

Quarter or halve potatoes. Heat a little olive oil in a heavy-based pan over high heat, add potatoes and toss to warm through and colour. Remove from pan and keep warm. Add a little more oil to pan, add bug tails and sear until just cooked.

To serve, combine watercress, rocket, pine nuts, onion and chives in a bowl and dress sparingly with lemon dressing. Mix roasted garlic mayonnaise through potatoes.

Centre potatoes on serving plates and top with three bug tails each, then dressed greens. Place one bug tail on top and drizzle with extra-virgin olive oil over and around. Season with black pepper and place a lemon wedge to one side.

See photograph page 49

At e'cco we favour warm salads as they suit our sub-tropical climate so well. Domestic cooks could save a lot of time and mess by buying the cuttlefish already cleaned. The cuttlefish may also be seared on the barbecue, if preferred. Squid (calamari) substitutes well for cuttlefish in this recipe, or you may like to use some shelled green (uncooked) prawns. Goan Cuisine in Western Australia produce a brilliant cucumber and chilli oil. It has an unbelievable golden orange hue and intense flavour but the oil may be difficult to obtain. I've given a recipe for chilli oil that works well in this dish.

Seared cuttlefish with cucumber, tomato, roast peppers and chilli oil

Serves 6 as a first course

chilli oil (Basics page 168)

1 red and 1 yellow pepper (capsicum), roasted, peeled and thickly sliced (Basics page 166)

600g (1 lb 5 oz) cuttlefish, medium sized

salad

1 continental cucumber, peeled

3 vine-ripened tomatoes

1 red onion, thinly sliced

1 cup coriander leaves

3 limes, juice only

salt/pepper

2 tablespoons olive oil

1 cup (150g/5 oz) peanuts, roasted

3 limes, halved

Prepare chilli oil and roasted peppers as recipes direct.

Prepare cuttlefish by slicing lengthwise through body. Open body and remove insides, including the cuttle bone. Pull skin away from flesh and discard with the tentacles. Using a very sharp knife, score the flesh into a diamond pattern, cutting not quite through.

To make the salad, use a mandoline (see Glossary) or vegetable peeler to shave cucumber into ribbons on four sides down to the seeds, discard seeds. Halve tomatoes horizontally, then cut into quarters. Combine cucumber, tomatoes, roasted peppers, onion and coriander leaves in a bowl and toss with chilli oil to taste. Add lime juice and season well with salt and black pepper.

To serve, heat a heavy-based pan (or barbecue) over high heat and add olive oil. Add cuttlefish, scored side down, and quickly sear until slightly coloured on both sides. Place two pieces of cuttlefish on each serving plate. Toss peanuts through salad and divide between plates, then top with a third piece of cuttlefish. Drizzle over a little extra chilli oil and serve with half a lime.

See photograph page 31

Queensland scallops are quite small and sweet with grey roe that is usually removed. This dish is best prepared using only scallop flesh without roe. A variation on this recipe is to quickly sear the unmarinated scallops.

Rice wine marinated scallops, spiced avocado and gazpacho

Serves 6 as a first course

gazpacho

1 small clove garlic, crushed
6 large, vine-ripened tomatoes, roughly chopped
1/2 red onion, diced
1 large orange, peeled, seeded and chopped
1 red pepper (capsicum), seeded and roughly chopped
1 cucumber, peeled and diced
1/2 cup (125ml/4 1/2 fl oz) olive oil
90ml (3 fl oz) lemon juice
1 1/2 cups (375ml/13 fl oz) tomato juice
1 tablespoon sherry vinegar
sea salt
cayenne pepper

2 limes, juice only
2 tablespoons rice wine vinegar
2 teaspoons pickled ginger with juice, finely chopped
dash thai fish sauce
freshly ground black pepper
18 scallops, trimmed of roe
spiced avocado (Side Dishes page 118)
1/2 cup coriander leaves

To make gazpacho, place garlic and tomatoes in an electric blender. Add onion, orange, red pepper and cucumber, blend until smooth. With machine running, drizzle in olive oil and lemon juice. Add tomato juice and sherry vinegar, mix, then strain into a bowl. Season with salt and cayenne pepper. Chill until needed.

For the scallops, combine lime juice, rice wine vinegar, pickled ginger, fish sauce and a generous grind of black pepper in a bowl. Slice each scallop across the grain into three discs. Add scallops to mixture and marinate for 30 minutes or until scallops are opaque.

To serve, prepare spiced avocado as recipe directs. Use an egg ring to shape a disc of avocado mixture in the centre of each serving plate, then carefully lift off egg ring. Spoon gazpacho around the perimeter. Remove scallops from marinade and arrange 9 discs, slightly overlapping, on top of spiced avocado. Garnish with coriander leaves.

See photograph page 49

We rarely use prepared products at e'cco, however the wakame sesame salad lends itself well to this dish. It's a delicious combination of shredded seaweed, chilli, sesame oil and sesame seed imported from Japan and distributed in Brisbane by Black Pearl Caviar. Chinese or Japanese pickled ginger is readily available but we prefer to use the locally produced Buderim pickled ginger. You may need to sear scallops in batches to keep a high temperature in the pan, otherwise scallops will lose a lot of liquid and begin to simmer rather than sear.

Seared scallops with wakame, coriander, cucumber and lime

Serves 4 as a first course

100g (3½ oz) caster sugar
100ml (3½ fl oz) water
2 coriander roots and stems
1 teaspoon thai fish sauce
2 continental cucumbers, peeled
100g (3½ oz) wakame sesame salad
90g (3 oz) watercress
1 cup coriander leaves
1 cup basil leaves
80g (3 oz) pickled ginger, shredded
2 limes, juice only
¼ cup (60ml/2 fl oz) peanut oil
400g (13 oz) fresh scallops, with or without roe
¼ cup (40g/1½ oz) sesame seed, roasted
2 limes, halved

Place sugar and water in a small saucepan and heat gently, stirring until sugar dissolves. Bring to the boil, boil for 5 minutes, then remove from heat. Crush coriander roots and stems to help release flavour before adding them to the syrup. Allow to cool, then stir in fish sauce.

Using a mandoline (see Glossary) or vegetable peeler, shave cucumbers into ribbons on four sides down to the seeds, discard seeds. Place in a bowl and add wakame sesame salad, watercress, fresh coriander and basil leaves and pickled ginger. Add lime juice and the strained flavoured syrup and mix lightly.

Heat peanut oil in a heavy-based pan over very high heat. Add scallops and quickly sear until cooked – they should take about 10 seconds each side.

To serve, reserve 8 scallops and divide the balance, centring them on serving plates. Top with salad and arrange two of the reserved scallops on top. Sprinkle with roasted sesame seed and garnish with half a lime.

See photograph page 30

Green peppercorn dressing is best used on the day it is made as, with all citrus-based dressings, it will lose freshness quickly. This intense and lively dressing is one of my favourites.

Grilled quail with crisp pear and green peppercorn dressing

Serves 4 as a first course

4 large quail, boned
2 tablespoons olive oil

green peppercorn dressing

2 tablespoons green peppercorns, with juice
1 clove garlic, crushed
1 teaspoon caster sugar
1 teaspoon worcestershire sauce (preferably Lee and Perrin)
1/2 cup (125ml/4 1/2 fl oz) extra-virgin olive oil
2 lemons, juice only
salt/pepper
2 tablespoons water

salad

60g (2 oz) rocket
1 small fennel bulb, finely diced
1 crisp pear, halved, cored and thinly sliced
1 yellow pepper (capsicum), roasted, peeled and thickly sliced (Basics page 164)
1 witlof (belgian endive), leaves separated
1 small red onion, thinly sliced into rings

To make the dressing, place peppercorns with their liquid in a food processor and pulse briefly to crush. Add garlic, sugar, worcestershire sauce, olive oil, lemon juice and blend well. Remove from processor, season with salt and black pepper. Whisk in water to thin.

Preheat oven to 200°C (400°F/Gas 6). Heat a heavy-based ovenproof frying pan over high heat. Brush quail with olive oil, season with salt and black pepper and place, skin side down, in pan to sear until a good colour is achieved. Turn quail over and place pan in preheated oven. Roast for 4-5 minutes. Remove quail from oven and allow to rest while assembling the salad.

Place rocket in a large bowl with fennel, pear, roasted pepper, witlof, onion and toss with just enough of the dressing to moisten.

To serve, quarter the warm quail. Place quail breasts on each serving plate and top with one-quarter of the salad. Sit quail legs on top of salad and drizzle a little dressing over and around the plate.

Our basic shank recipe calls for eight shanks. For this salad, one shank per person is sufficient.

Salad of veal shank, roast garlic, beetroot and red wine vinegar

serves 6 as a first course

braised veal shanks (Basics page 178)
red wine vinaigrette (Basics page 171)
1 head garlic confit (Basics page 167)
1 red onion, thinly sliced
1 cup (125g/4½ oz) ligurian olives (see Glossary)
flat-leaf parsley leaves
3 heads baby cos lettuce

pickled beetroot

12 baby beetroot, washed, stalks trimmed
¼ cup (60ml/2 fl oz) red wine vinegar (see Glossary)
½ cup (125g/4½ oz) lightly packed brown sugar
I bay leaf

Prepare braised shanks as recipe directs prior to reducing stock. Remove meat from cooled shanks in large pieces and refrigerate in stock until needed. This may be done up to three days ahead. Prepare red wine vinaigrette and garlic confit as recipes direct.

For the beetroot, place unpeeled beetroot in a heavy-based saucepan with the vinegar, brown sugar and bay leaf. Cover with cold water and bring to the boil. Reduce heat and simmer until tender. Drain, cool, peel and halve.

To serve, remove meat from stock and dice into 2.5cm (1 in) cubes. Return to stock and simmer until meat is well heated through. Remove hot meat from stock using a slotted spoon and place in a large bowl. Squeeze flesh from garlic confit into meat. Add beetroot, onion, olives, parsley leaves and mix lightly with enough of the vinaigrette to moisten. Place a few cos leaves on each serving plate. Divide salad between plates, resting on top of the cos leaves.

Rose Gray, of London's River Cafe, uses this method of blanching and not refreshing some vegetables as she believes too much flavour is lost in the refreshing process. I tend to agree. When using this method, do not prepare vegetables too far ahead as they do not hold well. They should be kept at room temperature after blanching for maximum flavour and seasoned with olive oil, salt and black pepper.

Salad of cornfed chicken, roast peppers and swiss chard

Serves 6 as a first course

12 oven-roasted tomato halves (Basics page 165)

1 red and 1 yellow pepper (capsicum), roasted, peeled and thickly sliced (Basics page 164)

1 x 2kg (4 lb 6 oz) cornfed chicken

salt/pepper

150g (5 oz) young swiss chard (silverbeet)

100g (3½ oz) french beans, trimmed and blanched

½ red onion, shaved

½ cup (75g/2½ oz) ligurian olives (see Glossary)

1 tablespoon salted capers, well rinsed

1 head garlic confit (Basics page 167)

½ cup (125ml/4½ fl oz) extra-virgin olive oil

1-2 lemons, juice only

Prepare oven-roasted tomatoes and roasted peppers as recipes direct.

Preheat oven to 180°C (350°F/Gas 4). Season chicken with salt and black pepper and place, breast side up, in a roasting pan. Roast for 1 hour, remove from oven and allow to rest for 10 minutes before serving.

Rinse chard, remove stems then blanch in well-salted boiling water. Drain but *do not* refresh in cold water. Spread leaves out on a clean kitchen cloth, drizzle with a little extra-virgin olive oil and season with salt and black pepper. Allow to rest at room temperature until needed.

Place roasted tomatoes and peppers in a large bowl. Add blanched chard, beans, onion, olives and capers. Squeeze garlic confit into the ½ cup olive oil and whisk to incorporate, adding enough lemon juice to balance flavours. Mix garlic dressing through salad.

To serve, divide salad between serving plates. Top with sliced chicken breast and thigh.

If time is short you can use a roasted duck bought from Chinatown.

Salad of slow-cooked duck, spinach, apple and hazelnuts

Serves 4 as a first course

red wine vinaigrette (Basics page 171)
4 slow-cooked duck thigh-and-leg portions (Basics page 177)
4 green (spring) onions, thinly sliced
125g (4½ oz) baby english spinach, stems removed
125g (4½ oz) rocket, stems removed
1 granny smith apple, quartered, cored and sliced
1 red onion, thinly sliced
1 cup (140g/5 oz) hazelnuts, roasted, skinned and roughly chopped
salt/pepper

Prepare red wine vinaigrette and slow-cooked duck as recipes direct, or remove skin and flesh from Chinese-style roasted duck.

Reserve 4 large pieces of the duck for garnish, slice remainder into smaller pieces and place in a large bowl. Reserve half the green onions for garnish and add remainder to duck with the spinach, rocket, apple, onion and hazelnuts. Add enough of the vinaigrette to moisten and toss through. Season with salt and black pepper.

To serve, divide salad between individual shallow bowls. Scatter reserved onion over and sit reserved duck pieces on the top.

Salad of chorizo, warm southern golds, peppers and soft poached egg

Serves 6 as a first course

balsamic dressing (Basics page 171)

1 roasted red pepper (capsicum), peeled, seeded and thickly sliced (Basics page 164)

250g (9 oz) french beans, trimmed

100g (3½ oz) rocket, stems removed

1 red onion, thinly sliced

18 small southern gold (pink-eye) potatoes, washed

6 soft poached eggs (Basics page 165)

olive oil, for cooking

6 fresh chorizo sausages

extra-virgin olive oil

freshly ground black pepper

Prepare balsamic dressing and roasted pepper as recipes direct.

Drop beans into a saucepan of boiling salted water and blanch 2 minutes. Drain and refresh in iced water, then drain again and hold at room temperature in a large bowl with the pepper, rocket and onion. Boil potatoes until just tender, drain and reserve.

Prepare soft poached eggs as recipe directs. Meanwhile, heat a heavy-based pan over moderate heat with a little olive oil and fry chorizo. Half-way through cooking, add halved, cooked potatoes and continue to fry until crisp.

To serve, thickly slice chorizo on the diagonal and arrange with potatoes in centre of each plate. Dress the bean mixture with enough balsamic dressing to moisten and arrange on top of sausage and potato. Place a poached egg on top of each salad and drizzle with a little extra-virgin olive oil. Finish with a grinding of black pepper.

Grilled quail, witlof, watercress, orange and pecans

Serves 4 as a first course

burnt orange vinaigrette (Basics page 172)
4 navel oranges, seedless
4 large quail, boned
2 tablespoons olive oil
salt/pepper
1 witlof (belgian endive), leaves separated
60g (2 oz) rocket, stems removed
40g (1½ oz) watercress
¾ cup (75g/2½ oz) pecans, roasted

Prepare burnt orange vinaigrette as recipe directs. Peel oranges removing all pith and slice into a total of sixteen 6mm (¼ in) thick rounds.

Preheat oven to 200°C (400°F/Gas 6). Heat a heavy-based ovenproof frying pan over high heat. Brush quail with olive oil, season with salt and black pepper and place, skin side down, in pan to sear until a good colour is achieved. Turn quail over and place pan in preheated oven. Roast for 4-5 minutes. Remove quail from oven and allow to rest while assembling the salad.

Place witlof in a large bowl with the rocket, watercress and pecans. Add just enough vinaigrette to moisten and lightly toss through.

To serve, quarter the warm quail. Arrange three slices of orange on each plate and top them with two quail breasts. Share salad between plates, sitting it on the quail. Top salad with final orange slice and quail legs. Drizzle a little extra vinaigrette over and around the plate.

See photograph page 50

Above right: Rice wine marinated scallops, spiced avocado and gazpacho (recipe page 41)

Right: Salad of bugs, pine nuts, red onion, southern golds and watercress (recipe page 39)

Left: Grilled quail, witlof, watercress, orange and pecans (recipe page 48)

Top: Risotto of spinach, pea, crisp prosciutto and shaved parmesan (recipe page 59)

Above: Risotto of duck, porcini mushrooms and spinach (recipe page 57)

risotto

Risotto of scallop, leek, saffron and vodka
Risotto of atlantic salmon, asparagus and parsley
Risotto of bug, fennel and chilli
Risotto of duck, porcini mushrooms and spinach
Risotto of pumpkin and goat's cheese
Risotto of spinach, pea, crisp prosciutto and shaved parmesan

Left: Risotto of bug, fennel and chilli (recipe page 56)

In a busy restaurant it is virtually impossible to cook a risotto from the start for each order. So the first recipe in this section shows a method where the rice is cooked almost completely, refrigerated and then finished off to order. Naturally, this cook-and-hold method applies to all risottos but it takes a bit of practice to stop the cooking process at just the right moment. If the rice is not cooked enough, it becomes very difficult to obtain the right texture when reconstituting. And, if initially overcooked, you end up with rice grains that are far too soft to be called risotto!

Risotto of scallop, leek, saffron and vodka

Serves 4 as a first course

2 tablespoons olive oil
1 tablespoon unsalted butter
2 leeks, sliced and well washed
4 shallots (french shallots), sliced
3 cloves garlic, sliced
large pinch saffron threads
1½ cups (330g/11½ oz) risotto rice (see Glossary)
1-1.2 litres (1¾-2 pt) chicken stock (Basics page 176), boiling
500g (17 oz) scallops
50g (2 oz) parmesan, freshly grated
2 tablespoons crème fraîche (see Glossary)
½ lemon, juice only
salt/pepper
basil leaves
vodka

Heat olive oil and butter in a heavy-based saucepan over moderate heat. Add leeks, shallots and garlic and gently sweat until shallots are transparent. Add saffron and rice to pan, stirring until rice is well coated with oil.

Reduce heat to low and add 1 cup (250ml/9 fl oz) of the boiling stock. Stir briefly and allow risotto to cook until the stock is almost completely absorbed by the rice. Add another 1 cup (250ml/9 fl oz) stock, stir and continue to cook until stock is almost absorbed. Continue adding stock and cooking in this way, stirring frequently, until rice is just undercooked. On a large tray, spread risotto in a thin layer to cool quickly. When cool, seal with plastic food wrap and refrigerate. Par-cooked risotto will keep up to 24 hours.

To serve, heat 1-2 cups (250-500ml/9-18 fl oz) chicken stock in a heavy-based saucepan over moderate heat. Add the par-cooked risotto and bring to the boil, stirring until stock is absorbed and rice is al dente. Add the scallops and cook until scallops are just opaque, then fold in parmesan, crème fraîche and lemon juice. Season well with salt and black pepper and fold through basil leaves. Spoon into shallow bowls and drizzle with vodka.

Risotto of atlantic salmon, asparagus and parsley

Serves 4 as a first course

$2\frac{1}{2}$ tablespoons (50ml/2 fl oz) olive oil

$2\frac{1}{2}$ tablespoons (50g/2 oz) unsalted butter

4 shallots (french shallots), diced

2 cloves garlic, finely chopped

$1\frac{1}{2}$ cups (330g/$11\frac{1}{2}$ oz) risotto rice (see Glossary)

1-1.2 litres ($1\frac{3}{4}$-2 pt) chicken stock (Basics page 176), boiling

440g (15 oz) fresh young asparagus

150g (5 oz) atlantic salmon, cut into 2cm ($\frac{3}{4}$ in) cubes

50g (2 oz) parmesan, freshly grated

salt/pepper

$\frac{1}{2}$ cup flat-leaf parsley, chopped

I lemon, juice only

Heat olive oil and half the butter in a heavy-based saucepan over moderate heat, add shallots and cook for 5 minutes. Toss in garlic and cook a further 3 minutes. Add rice and stir until rice is well coated with oil.

Reduce heat to low, add 1 cup (250ml/9 fl oz) of the boiling stock and stir briefly. Allow risotto to cook and the stock to be almost completely absorbed by the rice before adding another 1 cup (250ml/9 fl oz) stock, then stir again. Continue adding stock and cooking in this way, stirring frequently, until rice is almost cooked, about 15-20 minutes.

To serve, remove the woody ends from asparagus, peel stalks if needed and cut spears into thirds. Add asparagus and diced salmon to risotto – the heat from the rice is sufficient to cook the fish. Gently stir through parmesan and remaining butter and season, if needed, with salt and black pepper. Stir through parsley and lemon juice. Serve immediately in shallow bowls.

It was when Rick Stein, judge for Australian Gourmet Traveller *Restaurant of the Year in 1997, began to describe the food of the winning restaurant with this recipe for bug risotto, I realised e'cco had won! Moreton bay bugs are similar to Sydney's Balmain bugs with sweet, tender, white flesh. 'Bugs' are also known as shovelnose lobster or southern bay lobster. Uncooked crayfish or prawns also work well in this dish. Alternatively, if you wish to substitute with the flesh of cooked blue swimmer crabs or sandcrabs, add about 350g (12 oz) crabmeat immediately prior to serving as no extra cooking is required.*

Risotto of bug, fennel and chilli

Serves 4 as a first course

500g (17 oz) uncooked moreton bay or balmain bug meat
2 tablespoons olive oil
2½ tablespoons (50g/2 oz) unsalted butter
1 fennel bulb, sliced and washed
4 shallots (french shallots) or 1 onion, diced
2 cloves garlic, crushed
2 teaspoons fennel seed, roasted and ground
½ teaspoon dried chilli flakes
salt/pepper
1½ cups (330g/11½ oz) risotto rice (see Glossary)
1-1.2 litres (1¾-2 pt) chicken stock (Basics page 176), boiling
50g (2 oz) parmesan, freshly grated
1 lemon, juice only
3 tablespoons flat-leaf parsley, finely chopped
shaved parmesan
lemon oil (see Glossary)

Cut bug tails into 2cm (¾ in) medallions and set aside. Heat oil and half the butter in a heavy-based saucepan over moderate heat. Add fennel bulb, shallots, garlic, fennel seed, chilli and gently sweat until shallots are transparent. Lightly season with salt and black pepper. Add rice and stir until rice is well coated with oil.

Reduce heat to low, add 1 cup (250ml/9 fl oz) of the boiling stock and stir briefly. Allow risotto to cook and the stock to be almost completely absorbed by the rice before adding another 1 cup (250ml/9 fl oz) stock, then stir again. Continue adding stock and cooking in this way, stirring frequently, until rice is almost cooked, about 15-20 minutes.

Add the bug medallions to risotto and gently heat until just cooked through. Fold through grated parmesan, remaining butter, lemon juice to taste and the parsley. Check seasonings and make sure the risotto is not too wet – increase heat and allow liquid to evaporate if it is.

To serve, spoon risotto into shallow bowls, top with shaved parmesan, drizzle with lemon oil and finish with a grinding of black pepper.

See photograph page 52

This is another recipe where you can substitute Chinese-style roast duck. The Slow-cooked Duck (Basics page 177) could also be folded through at the end of the cooking time.

Risotto of duck, porcini mushrooms and spinach

Serves 4 as a first course

75g (2½ oz) dried porcini mushrooms
2 x 1.5kg (3½ lb) roasted ducks
2 tablespoons olive oil
2½ tablespoons (50g/2 oz) unsalted butter
4 shallots (french shallots), diced
2 cloves garlic, finely chopped
1½ cups (330g/11½ oz) risotto rice (see Glossary)
1-1.2 litres (1¾-2 pt) chicken stock (Basics page 176), boiling
1 onion, diced
4 medium swiss brown mushrooms, thinly sliced
80g (3 oz) english spinach, stems removed
50g (2 oz) parmesan, freshly grated
salt/pepper
shaved parmesan
extra-virgin olive oil

Soak porcini in enough cold water to cover until softened, about 4 hours. Remove flesh and skin from duck and dice, discarding bones and fat.

Heat oil and half the butter in a heavy-based saucepan over moderate heat. Add shallots and garlic and gently sweat until shallots are transparent. Add rice and stir until rice is well coated with oil. Lift porcini from soaking water. Carefully strain liquid, avoiding any grit that will have settled in bottom of bowl, and stir both porcini and liquid through rice.

Reduce heat to low, add 1 cup (250ml/9 fl oz) of the boiling stock and stir briefly. Allow risotto to cook and the stock to be almost completely absorbed by the rice before adding another 1 cup (250ml/9 fl oz) stock, then stir again. Continue adding stock and cooking in this way, stirring frequently, until rice is almost cooked, about 15-20 minutes.

Meanwhile, in a separate saucepan, heat a little extra oil over moderate to high heat and sauté onion and fresh mushrooms, seasoning with salt and black pepper. Deglaze pan with 2 cups (500ml/18 fl oz) of the chicken stock, then pour mixture into rice and stir briefly. Continue cooking risotto until liquid is almost totally absorbed and rice is cooked al dente, then stir in duck and spinach. Heat through, add grated parmesan and remaining butter and adjust seasonings to taste. If you prefer a wetter risotto, add a little more hot stock.

To serve, spoon risotto into shallow bowls, top with shaved parmesan, a splash of extra-virgin olive oil and a good grinding of black pepper.

Risotto of pumpkin and goat's cheese

Serves 4 as a first course

1.5kg ($3\frac{1}{2}$ lb) butternut pumpkin (squash), peeled, seeded
3 tablespoons olive oil
4 cloves garlic, finely chopped
1.2 litres (2 pt) chicken stock (Basics page 176) or vegetable stock
$2\frac{1}{2}$ tablespoons (50g/2 oz) unsalted butter
1 onion, finely diced
4 shallots (french shallots), diced
$1\frac{1}{2}$ cups (330g/$11\frac{1}{2}$ oz) risotto rice (see Glossary)
$\frac{1}{2}$ cup oregano leaves
50g (2 oz) parmesan, freshly grated
salt/pepper
200g ($6\frac{1}{2}$ oz) log fresh goat's cheese

Julienne 1 cup (150g/5 oz) of the pumpkin, then dice remainder. Heat 2 tablespoons olive oil in a heavy-based saucepan over moderate heat, add the garlic and sweat briefly. Add the stock and diced pumpkin and bring to the boil. Reduce heat to low and simmer for 20 minutes or until pumpkin is soft. Purée pumpkin in stock, return to heat and bring to a simmer.

In a separate heavy-based saucepan, heat remaining oil and half the butter over moderate heat. Add onion and shallots and gently sweat until onion is transparent. Add rice and stir until rice is well coated with oil.

Reduce heat to low, add 1 cup (250ml/9 fl oz) of the boiling pumpkin stock and stir briefly. Allow risotto to cook and the stock to be almost completely absorbed by the rice before adding another 1 cup (250ml/9 fl oz) stock, then stir again. Continue adding stock and cooking in this way, stirring frequently, until rice is almost cooked, about 15-20 minutes. Stir through shredded pumpkin and continue cooking until pumpkin is tender – you may need to add a little additional stock.

To serve, stir in remaining butter, oregano leaves, parmesan and adjust seasonings to taste. Spoon into wide shallow bowls, topping each with a disc of goat's cheese and a grinding of black pepper.

Risotto of spinach, pea, crisp prosciutto and shaved parmesan

Serves 4 as a first course

12 slices shaved prosciutto
2 tablespoons olive oil
2½ tablespoons (50g/2 oz) unsalted butter
4 shallots (french shallots), diced
2 cloves garlic, finely chopped
1½ cups (330g/11½ oz) risotto rice (see Glossary)
1-1.2 litres (1¾-2 pt) chicken stock (Basics page 176), boiling
1 cup (200g/7 oz) puréed english spinach
2 cups (300g/10 oz) shelled green peas
50g (2 oz) parmesan, freshly grated
¼ cup (50g/2 oz) pesto (Basics page 166)
300g (10 oz) english spinach leaves, stems removed
salt/pepper
shaved parmesan
extra-virgin olive oil

Preheat oven to 200°C (400°F/Gas 6). Lay prosciutto in a single layer on an oven tray and bake until crisp.

Heat olive oil and half the butter in a heavy-based saucepan over moderate heat. Add shallots and garlic and gently sweat until shallots are transparent. Add rice and stir until rice is well coated with oil.

Reduce heat to low, add 1 cup (250ml/9 fl oz) of the boiling stock and stir briefly. Allow risotto to cook and the stock to be almost completely absorbed by the rice before adding another 1 cup (250ml/9 fl oz) stock, then stir again. Continue adding stock and cooking in this way, stirring frequently, until rice is almost cooked, about 15-20 minutes.

Add puréed spinach and peas to risotto and continue adding stock and cooking until rice is tender and creamy. Stir in grated parmesan, remaining butter and pesto. Lastly, stir in fresh spinach and season well with salt and black pepper.

To serve, spoon into wide shallow bowls and top with shaved parmesan, crisp prosciutto, a splash of extra-virgin olive oil and some freshly ground black pepper.

See photograph page 51

e'cco

pasta, gnocchi, pizza

Penne, bacon, garlic, chilli and rocket

Serves 6 as a first course

500g (17 oz) penne
1 tablespoon olive oil
4 shallots (french shallots), sliced
2 cloves garlic, crushed
pinch dried chilli flakes
18 thin rashers bacon, rindless
200g (7 oz) rocket, stems removed
100g (3 1/2 oz) parmesan, freshly grated
1/2 lemon, juice only
salt/pepper
shaved parmesan
extra-virgin olive oil

Bring a large saucepan of salted water to the boil. Add pasta and return to the boil, stirring to prevent sticking. Cook for 7-8 minutes or until pasta is al dente.

In a separate large saucepan, heat olive oil over moderate heat, add shallots, garlic and chilli and sauté until shallots are transparent. Grill bacon until crisp and add to the sauce.

When pasta is cooked, drain, return to saucepan and add the sauce, tossing to coat. Mix through rocket, grated parmesan and lemon juice. Season with salt and black pepper.

To serve, spoon into shallow bowls, top with shaved parmesan, drizzle with extra-virgin olive oil and season with more black pepper.

Penne, eggplant, tomato, olives and fetta

Serves 6 as a first course

600ml (21 fl oz) rich tomato sauce (Basics page 171)
2 small eggplant (aubergine), sliced in 2.5cm (1 in) thick rounds
extra-virgin olive oil
500g (17 oz) penne
1 tablespoon olive oil
1 tablespoon unsalted butter
3 shallots (french shallots), diced
3 cloves garlic, crushed
3/4 cup (100g/3 1/2 oz) ligurian olives (see Glossary)
salt/pepper
3/4 cup basil leaves
150g (5 oz) fetta

Prepare rich tomato sauce as recipe directs.

Brush eggplant slices on both sides with extra-virgin olive oil and grill until well-coloured and softened. Set aside. It is important to cook eggplant thoroughly or it will be tough.

Bring a large saucepan of salted water to the boil. Add pasta and return to the boil, stirring to prevent sticking. Cook for 7-8 minutes or until pasta is al dente.

Meanwhile, heat 1 tablespoon olive oil in a large saucepan, add the butter, shallots, garlic and sauté until shallots are transparent. Add rich tomato sauce, eggplant and olives, season with salt and black pepper.

When the pasta is cooked, drain and fold sauce through with torn basil leaves. To serve, spoon into shallow bowls and crumble fetta on top.

We have tried a number of potato varieties for gnocchi and find bintje, a waxy potato, works best. Gnocchi can be shaped and cooked in advance. Refresh in iced water, drain then drizzle with a little oil to prevent sticking, and store in the refrigerator until required. Gnocchi will keep 1-2 days.

Potato gnocchi

Serves 6 as a first course

750g (1 lb 10 oz) bintje potatoes, scrubbed
150g (5 oz) baker's flour (see Glossary)
1 egg, lightly beaten
50g (2 oz) parmesan, freshly grated
pinch of nutmeg, freshly grated
salt/pepper

Steam the potatoes until tender, cool a little, then peel and pass through a mouli or sieve – you should have 500g (17 oz) cooked potatoes. Fold flour into potatoes, then gently stir in the egg, parmesan and nutmeg. Season to taste with salt and black pepper. Do not overwork the mixture or gnocchi will be tough.

To shape gnocchi, roll mixture into cylindrical shapes 2.5cm (1 in) in diameter. Using a floured knife, cut diagonally into 2.5cm (1 in) lengths.

To serve, bring a large saucepan of salted water to a simmer. Add gnocchi and cook for 5-8 minutes or until they float – remove one and test. Gnocchi should be cooked in the centre and not gluey. Drain gnocchi, return to pan and coat with prepared sauce.

Crisp grilled bacon or pancetta gives added flavour and texture to this dish.

Potato gnocchi with gorgonzola, spinach and pine nuts

Serves 6 as a first course

potato gnocchi (page 63)
2 tablespoons olive oil
100g ($3\frac{1}{2}$ oz) shallots (french shallots), sliced
3 cloves garlic, sliced
$\frac{1}{2}$ cup (125ml/$4\frac{1}{2}$ fl oz) dry white wine
300ml (11 fl oz) cream
150-200g (5-7 oz) english spinach, stems removed
80g (3 oz) italian gorgonzola, fully matured, roughly chopped
$\frac{1}{2}$ lemon, juice only
salt/pepper
shaved parmesan
$\frac{1}{4}$ cup (40g/$1\frac{1}{2}$ oz) pine nuts, roasted

Shape and cook gnocchi as recipe directs.

Heat the olive oil in a heavy-based pan over moderate heat and sauté shallots and garlic until soft but not coloured. Deglaze the pan with wine, simmering until it reduces by half. Add cream to pan and continue to simmer until mixture reduces by one-third. Add spinach, gorgonzola and lemon juice, season with salt and black pepper and adjust to taste.

To serve, cook gnocchi as directed, drain, add to the sauce and mix lightly. Spoon into shallow bowls, top with shaved parmesan and scatter with pine nuts.

Fresh goat's curd has a milder flavour and softer texture than goat's cheese. You can substitute with goat's cheese if the curd is not readily available.

Potato gnocchi, balsamic, tomato, basil and goat's curd

Serves 6 as a first course

potato gnocchi (page 63)
600ml (21 fl oz) rich tomato sauce (Basics page 171)
100ml (3½ fl oz) best quality balsamic vinegar
50g (2½ tablespoons) unsalted butter
1 cup basil leaves
250g (9 oz) fresh goat's curd
extra-virgin olive oil
freshly ground black pepper

Shape and cook the gnocchi and prepare rich tomato sauce as recipes direct.

Place balsamic vinegar in a large, heavy-based saucepan and bring to the boil. Boil until vinegar becomes syrupy – the time is dependent on the quality of the balsamic used. Whisk in the butter, then stir in the rich tomato sauce. Return sauce to the boil, taste and adjust seasonings.

To serve, cook gnocchi as directed, drain, add to the balsamic tomato sauce with the torn basil leaves and mix lightly. Spoon into shallow bowls, top with a spoonful of goat's curd and finish with a drizzle of extra-virgin olive oil and freshly ground black pepper.

If time is short, your local pizzeria will probably sell you some pizza dough. However I prefer to always make my own. I have yet to find a par-cooked commercial pizza base that I would like to eat. If the ambient temperature is warm, use iced water instead of warm water to slow the rising of the dough. Having the dough slowly rise, allows time for flavours to develop. If baker's flour is unavailable, use plain flour with 10 percent gluten flour added.

Pizza dough

Makes two 28cm (11 in) or four 20cm (8 in) pizza bases

$1\frac{1}{2}$ teaspoons dry yeast
150-175ml (5-6 fl oz) water, just warm
225g (8 oz) baker's flour (see Glossary)
pinch of sugar
2 tablespoons extra-virgin olive oil
$\frac{1}{2}$ teaspoon salt

Whisk yeast with $\frac{1}{4}$ cup (60ml/2 fl oz) of the water, $\frac{1}{4}$ cup (30g/1 oz) of the flour and sugar in bowl of electric mixer. Stand 30 minutes and allow yeast to activate. This ensures yeast is still alive.

Add oil, salt and remaining flour to frothy mixture, kneading with dough hook, and adding enough water to make a sticky dough. You may need to add a little more water, depending on moisture content of the flour. Continue to knead until dough is smooth and elastic. Seal bowl with plastic food wrap, stand in a warm place and allow the dough to rise until doubled in size.

Remove dough to a heavily floured surface. Divide dough into two or four equal pieces and roll into balls. Lightly oil pizza trays. Using floured hands or rolling pin, flatten dough to fit pizza trays and allow to rest while organising the desired topping. Top pizza, then bake as directed in recipes.

Pizza of southern golds, rosemary, taleggio and truffle oil

pizza dough (page 66)
12 small southern gold (pink-eye) potatoes, scrubbed
1 teaspoon rosemary, chopped
2 cloves garlic, crushed
1 tablespoon extra-virgin olive oil
200g (7 oz) taleggio, sliced (see Glossary)
truffle oil (see Glossary)
freshly ground black pepper

Prepare pizza dough as recipe directs.

Steam the potatoes until tender, cool, then slice thickly. Preheat oven to highest setting – 250°C (500°F/Gas 9).

Combine rosemary, garlic and olive oil then brush over pizza bases. Top with potato slices and bake for 10 minutes.

Remove pizza from oven, then top with taleggio, return to oven for several minutes or until cheese melts and crust is cooked. Drizzle with truffle oil and season with black pepper. Serve pizzas with a green salad.

Pizza of fresh fig, prosciutto and taleggio

pizza dough (page 66)
rich tomato sauce (Basics page 171)
lemon dressing (Basics page 172)
4 fresh figs, quartered
200g (7 oz) taleggio, sliced (see Glossary)
60g (2 oz) rocket, stems removed
8 slices prosciutto
freshly ground black pepper

Prepare pizza dough, rich tomato sauce and lemon dressing as recipes direct.

Preheat oven to highest setting – 250°C (500°F/Gas 9). Half-cook pizza bases (7-10 minutes) then remove from oven and spread lightly with rich tomato sauce. Top pizza with figs and taleggio. Return pizzas to oven and bake for 7-10 minutes or until crust is cooked through.

To serve, lightly dress rocket with lemon dressing. Drape pizzas with sliced prosciutto and top with the rocket. Season with freshly ground black pepper.

Pizza with caramelised onion, gorgonzola, pear and walnut

pizza dough (page 66)
caramelised onion (onion jam/Basics page 173)
red wine vinaigrette (Basics page 171)
200g (7 oz) italian gorgonzola, fully matured roughly chopped
2 pears, cored and cut into thin wedges
1 red onion, thinly sliced into rings
60g (2 oz) rocket, stems removed
1/2 cup (60g/2 oz) walnuts (preferably californian), roasted

Prepare pizza dough, onion jam and red wine vinaigrette as recipes direct.

Preheat oven to highest setting – 250°C (500°F/Gas 9). Thinly spread onion jam over pizza bases and bake for 10 minutes. Top onion jam with gorgonzola and bake a further 5-8 minutes. Remove from oven.

In mixing bowl, combine pears, onion, rocket and walnuts with enough of the vinaigrette to moisten. Top each pizza with a portion of the salad.

Right: Pizza with caramelised onion, gorgonzola, pear and walnut (recipe this page)

Above: Atlantic salmon with panzanella (recipe page 75)

Right: Snapper with green tomatoes, slow-cooked fennel and flat-leaf parsley (recipe page 80)

fish, seafood

Rare tuna, asparagus, frisee, artichoke and soft poached egg
Atlantic salmon with panzanella
Atlantic salmon, spiced avocado and burnt orange vinaigrette
Coral trout, roasted jerusalem artichoke and carrot with crushed green chilli
Atlantic salmon, corncake, crème fraîche, date and lime chutney
Barramundi with champ, soft poached egg and capers
Whiting fillets with cos, anchovy mayo and tapenade crostini
Snapper with green tomatoes, slow-cooked fennel and flat-leaf parsley
Blue eye cod, chilli tomato compote, saffron and zucchini
Snapper, pickled eggplant, basil and rocket
Pearl perch, chilli saffron tomatoes and asparagus

Left: Blue eye cod, chilli tomato compote, saffron and zucchini (recipe page 81)

Rare tuna, asparagus, frisee, artichoke and soft poached egg

Serves 6 as a main course

lemon dressing (Basics page 172)

18 asparagus spears, trimmed and halved diagonally

6 soft poached eggs (Basics page 165)

hollandaise (Basics page 168)

6 x 180g (6 oz) tuna or swordfish steaks

salt/pepper

1 tablespoon olive oil

12 artichoke hearts, halved (preferably with stems)

1/4 cup flat-leaf parsley

90g (3 oz) frisee lettuce (young curly endive)

1/2 red onion, thinly sliced into rings

6 lemon wedges

Prepare lemon dressing as recipe directs. Blanch asparagus in boiling salted water, refresh in iced water. Poach eggs and prepare hollandaise as recipes direct and keep warm.

Season fish on both sides with salt and black pepper. Heat a heavy-based pan over high heat, add the olive oil and sear fish 3-4 minutes each side until medium-rare. Remove from pan and allow to rest 3-5 minutes – remember the fish will continue to cook while cooling.

Reheat the cleaned pan over high heat and add a little olive oil. Add drained asparagus and artichoke hearts, toss well to colour and heat through, fold through parsley, season to taste with salt and black pepper.

Combine frisee lettuce and onion in a bowl and toss with just enough lemon dressing to moisten.

To serve, place salad on serving plates with a lemon wedge to one side. Top salad with asparagus and artichokes, the fish, then poached egg. Coat egg with hollandaise.

Atlantic salmon with panzanella

Serves 6 as a main course

panzanella (Side Dishes page 122)

6 x 180g (6 oz) salmon portions, skin on, scaled and pin boned (see Glossary)

salt/pepper

1 tablespoon olive oil

lemon wedges

Prepare panzanella as recipe directs.

Season salmon skin with salt and black pepper. Heat a heavy-based (or non-stick) pan over high heat and add the olive oil. Place salmon in pan, skin side down, and sear until a good colour is achieved. Reduce heat to moderate, turn salmon and cook a further 3-5 minutes, or until medium-rare.

To serve, place a large spoonful of panzanella in each wide, shallow bowl. Lay a salmon portion on top and garnish with a lemon wedge.

See photograph page 70

Atlantic salmon, spiced avocado and burnt orange vinaigrette

Serves 6 as a main course

spiced avocado (Side Dishes page 118)

burnt orange vinaigrette (Basics page 172)

6 x 180g (6 oz) atlantic salmon portions, skin on, scaled and pin boned (see Glossary)

salt/pepper

olive oil

½ cup (75g/2½ oz) whole blanched almonds, roasted

coriander leaves

12 anchovy fillets in oil, drained and sliced lengthwise

2 tablespoons salted capers, well rinsed

3 limes, halved

Prepare spiced avocado and burnt orange vinaigrette as recipes direct.

Season salmon skin with salt and black pepper. Heat a heavy-based (or non-stick) frying pan over high heat and add a little olive oil. Add salmon to pan, skin side down, and sear until a good colour is achieved. Reduce heat to moderate, turn salmon and cook a further 3-5 minutes or until medium-rare.

To serve, place a large spoonful of spiced avocado onto plates. Sprinkle with roasted almonds, coriander leaves, anchovies and capers. Drizzle vinaigrette on and around the avocado mix. Place a salmon portion on top, skin side up, and serve with half a lime.

Coral trout, roasted jerusalem artichoke and carrot with crushed green chilli

Serves 6 as a main course

olive oil, for cooking
12 jerusalem artichokes, peeled
6 small carrots, sliced diagonally
2 teaspoons fennel seed
salt/pepper
6 x 180g (6 oz) coral trout fillets (skinless, boneless)
½ cup (60g/2 oz) plain flour
250g (9 oz) young swiss chard (silverbeet), stems removed
3 limes, halved

chilli lemon dressing

1 fresh green chilli, seeded and finely diced
I lemon, grated zest only
¼ cup (60ml/2 fl oz) extra-virgin olive oil

For the dressing, place chilli and lemon zest in a bowl, then whisk in the extra-virgin olive oil – this dressing is best allowed to infuse for several hours.

Preheat oven to 180°C (350°F/Gas 4). Heat a heavy-based, ovenproof frying pan over high heat and add a little olive oil. Add artichokes, carrots and fennel seed, season with salt and black pepper and toss over heat for several minutes until coloured. Place pan in oven and roast vegetables until tender.

Dust fish lightly with flour, shake off excess. Season both sides with salt and pepper. Heat an ovenproof heavy-based (or non-stick) pan over high heat, add a little olive oil and sear fish on one side until golden. Turn fish then place pan in oven and cook approximately 8 minutes – fish should be cooked but still moist. Meanwhile, season chard and sauté in a separate pan in a little olive oil until wilted.

To serve, place roasted vegetables and chard into centre of serving plates and top with fish portions. Drizzle chilli lemon dressing over and around plate and garnish with half a lime.

Atlantic salmon, corncake, crème fraîche, date and lime chutney

Serves 6 as a main course

date and lime chutney (Basics page 174)

chilli corncakes (Side Dishes page 120)

6 x 180g (6 oz) atlantic salmon portions, skin on, scaled and pin boned (see Glossary)

salt/pepper

olive oil

400g (13 oz) baby english spinach leaves, stems removed

crème fraîche (see Glossary)

3 limes, halved

Prepare date and lime chutney and chilli corncakes as recipes direct.

Season salmon skin with salt and black pepper. Heat a heavy-based (or non-stick) frying pan over high heat and add a little olive oil. Sear salmon, skin side down, until a good colour is achieved. Reduce heat to moderate, turn salmon and cook a further 3-5 minutes or until medium-rare.

In a separate pan, season spinach and sauté in a little hot oil until just wilted.

To serve, centre a warm corncake on each serving plate and top with salmon, skin side up. Place spinach alongside, then finish with a spoonful each of crème fraîche and date and lime chutney. Garnish with half a lime.

Barramundi with champ, soft poached egg and capers

Serves 6 as a main course

6 soft poached eggs (Basics page 165)
champ (Side Dishes page 120)
6 x 180g (6 oz) barramundi (or use blue eye cod or turbot) portions, (skinless, boneless)
1/2 cup (60g/2 oz) plain flour
1/2 cup (125ml/4 1/2 fl oz) clarified butter (Basics page 164)

lemon and caper sauce

1 whole salted lemon (Basics page 173)
1 tablespoon unsalted butter
1 tablespoon salted capers, well rinsed
1/2 cup flat-leaf parsley
1/2 lemon, juice only
salt/pepper

Prepare salted lemons for the sauce, poach eggs and prepare champ as recipes direct.

To make the lemon and caper sauce, heat butter in a small saucepan over moderate heat until nut brown in colour. Remove and discard flesh from the salted lemon, then dice finely. Add to saucepan with the capers, parsley and lemon juice. Taste and adjust seasonings, if required. Keep warm.

Preheat grill to high. Lightly dust fish with flour and shake off excess. Place on greased oven tray and brush tops with clarified butter. Season with salt and black pepper. Grill approximately 8 minutes until cooked but still moist.

To serve, place a large spoonful of champ on each serving plate. Sit fish on champ and top with a warm poached egg. Spoon over lemon and caper sauce.

Whiting fillets with cos, anchovy mayo and tapenade crostini

Serves 6 as a main course

3 tablespoons tapenade (Basics page 166)

900g (2 lb) whiting fillets, scaled, skin on

1 cup (125g/4½ oz) plain flour

½ cup (125ml/4½ fl oz) clarified butter, melted (Basics page 164)

salt/pepper

6 x 2.5cm (1 in) thick slices ciabatta or other italian bread (see Glossary)

3 small cos lettuces

lemon wedges

anchovy mayo

1 quantity roasted garlic mayonnaise (Basics page 167)

8 anchovy fillets in oil, drained and chopped

Prepare tapenade as recipe directs. To make anchovy mayo, prepare roasted garlic mayonnaise, then fold in the anchovies.

Preheat grill to hot. Lightly dust whiting fillets with the flour and shake off excess. Place on greased oven tray, skin side up. Brush with clarified butter, then season with salt and black pepper. Grill until good colour is achieved, approximately 5-8 minutes.

Toast ciabatta and spread lightly with tapenade.

To serve, remove and discard outer leaves from cos, halve, then wash and shake dry. Trim core, leaving just enough to hold leaves together. Centre half a cos on each plate, cut side up. Lay whiting over base of lettuce and accompany with tapenade crostini, anchovy mayo and a lemon wedge.

Snapper with green tomatoes, slow-cooked fennel and flat-leaf parsley

Serves 6 as a main course

slow-cooked fennel (Side Dishes page 121)
150ml (5 fl oz) olive oil
3 cloves garlic, unpeeled, lightly crushed
8 medium green roma (italian plum) tomatoes, halved and seeded
2 cups (500ml/18 fl oz) chicken stock (Basics page 176)
100g (3½ oz) unsalted butter
1 cup (150g/5 oz) ligurian olives, pitted (see Glossary)
1 cup flat-leaf parsley
I lemon, juice only
salt/pepper
beurre blanc (Basics page 178)
6 x 180g (6 oz) snapper or sea-bass fillets (skin-on, boneless)
½ cup (60g/2 oz) plain flour
½ cup (125ml/4½ fl oz) clarified butter, melted (Basics page 164)

Prepare slow-cooked fennel as recipe directs.

Meanwhile, heat olive oil in a heavy-based saucepan over high heat. Add garlic and tomatoes – tomato skins should blister with the heat. Add half the chicken stock and cook until reduced by half. Add remaining stock and cook again until reduced by half – at this stage tomatoes should be cooked through. Remove tomatoes with a slotted spoon and set aside.

Add butter to pan and cook until juices are reduced to a syrupy consistency. Add slow-cooked fennel, olives and parsley leaves, season with lemon juice, salt and black pepper.

Meanwhile, prepare beurre blanc and keep warm.

Preheat grill to hot. Slash skin diagonally several times. Dip fish into flour and shake off excess. Place fish in single layer, skin side up on greased oven tray. Brush lightly with clarified butter, season well with salt and black pepper. Grill until just cooked, approximately 8 minutes.

To serve, divide warm tomatoes, fennel and olives between serving plates or wide, shallow bowls. Top with grilled fish, drizzle with beurre blanc.

See photograph page 71

The chilli dressing is quite hot. If you would like to lessen the heat, remove seeds and inner ribs from chillies before slicing. The dressing should be balanced with distinctive hot, sweet and sour flavours.

Blue eye cod, chilli tomato compote, saffron and zucchini

Serves 6 as a main course

12 oven-roasted tomato halves (Basics page 165)

beurre blanc (Basics page 178)

pinch saffron threads

6 x 180g (6 oz) blue eye cod fillets (skinless, boneless)

1/2 cup (60g/2 oz) plain flour

1/2 cup (125ml/4 1/2 fl oz) clarified butter, melted (Basics page 164)

salt/pepper

6 medium zucchini (courgette)

1/2 cup coriander leaves

chilli and mustard seed dressing

2 tablespoons peanut oil

2 tablespoons black or brown mustard seed

1/3 cup (45g/1 1/2 oz) red chillies, sliced diagonally

1/3 cup (60-75g/2-2 1/2 oz) fresh ginger, peeled and finely julienned

2 cloves garlic, thinly sliced

1/2 cup (90g/3 oz) palm sugar

2 teaspoons thai fish sauce

6 limes, juice only

Prepare oven-roasted tomatoes. Prepare beurre blanc as recipe directs, except add the saffron threads with the cream, after straining. Keep sauce warm.

For the dressing, heat oil in a small saucepan until hot. Add mustard seed and cook for 2-3 minutes – they will begin to pop. Add chillies, ginger, garlic and cook for a further 2 minutes. Remove from heat and add palm sugar, fish sauce and lime juice to taste.

Preheat grill to hot. Coat fish fillets with flour and shake off the excess. Place fish on greased oven tray, brush with clarified butter and season with salt and black pepper. Grill fish until just cooked and golden, approximately 8 minutes.

Top and tail zucchini and julienne lengthwise. Heat a little clarified butter in a heavy-based pan over high heat and sauté the zucchini until tender. Season with salt and black pepper. Add the roasted tomatoes to one side of the pan and warm through.

To serve, divide zucchini between serving plates. Place fish on top and drizzle the saffron butter sauce around the perimeter. Place two warm tomato halves on fish and top with coriander leaves. Stir the dressing well and generously spoon over tomatoes.

See photograph page 72

Snapper, pickled eggplant, basil and rocket

Serves 6 as a main course

6 x 180g (6 oz) snapper or sea-bass fillets, skin on, scaled and boned
1/2 cup (60g/2 oz) plain flour
1/2 cup (125ml/4 1/2 fl oz) clarified butter, melted (Basics page 164)
90g (3 oz) rocket, stems removed
extra-virgin olive oil
lemon wedges

pickled eggplant (aubergine)

1 tablespoon olive oil
1/2 onion, diced
3 cloves garlic, crushed
1/4 cup (30-45g/1-1 1/2 oz) fresh ginger, peeled and finely julienned
3 green or red chillies, seeded and thinly sliced
1 teaspoon brown mustard seed
1 tablespoon cumin seed, roasted and ground
2 x 400g (13 oz) cans roma (italian plum) tomatoes, roughly chopped (including juice)
1/4 cup (60ml/2 fl oz) cider vinegar
1/2 cup (60g/2 oz) soft brown sugar
2 medium eggplant (aubergine), thickly sliced
clarified butter, melted (Basics page 164)
1 cup basil leaves
salt/pepper

For the eggplant, heat olive oil in a heavy-based saucepan over moderate heat and sweat the onion, garlic, ginger and chillies until onion is transparent. Add mustard seed and ground cumin and cook, stirring, until fragrant. Stir in tomatoes, the vinegar, sugar and bring to the boil. Reduce heat and simmer for 30 minutes, stirring often.

Preheat grill (or barbecue) until hot. Brush eggplant slices with a little clarified butter and grill until soft and well-coloured. Roughly chop eggplant and fold through tomato mixture with torn basil. Check and adjust seasonings. Serve at room temperature. Excess will keep several days in refrigerator.

To cook the fish, preheat grill to hot. Slash fish skin diagonally several times. Dip snapper fillets into flour, shake off excess, place on greased oven tray, brush with clarified butter then season with salt and black pepper. Grill fish for 5-8 minutes, depending on thickness, until cooked through.

To serve, place snapper on serving plates with a large spoonful of pickled eggplant to one side. Divide rocket between plates, drizzle with extra-virgin olive oil and accompany with a lemon wedge.

Pearl perch, chilli saffron tomatoes and asparagus

Serves 6 as a main course

600ml (21 fl oz) rich tomato sauce (Basics page 171)
2 medium red onions, peeled
olive oil, for cooking
2 red chillies, thinly sliced
good pinch saffron threads
salt/pepper
6 x 180g (6 oz) pearl perch fillets (boneless, skinless)
½ cup (60g/2 oz) plain flour
clarified butter, melted (Basics page 164)
18 thick asparagus spears, woody ends removed

Prepare rich tomato sauce as recipe directs.

Leaving root attached, halve then cut each onion into three wedges. Heat a little olive oil in a heavy-based saucepan over moderate heat, add onion wedges and sauté until they are coloured and begin to soften. Add chillies and saffron and cook for a further minute. Add rich tomato sauce and bring to the boil. Reduce heat and simmer for several minutes. Taste and adjust seasonings, if required.

Preheat grill to hot. Dust fish with flour, shake off excess. Place fish on greased oven tray, brush with clarified butter and season with salt and black pepper. Grill fish until just cooked, approximately 8 minutes.

To serve, blanch asparagus in boiling salted water until just tender and drain. Spoon tomato chilli saffron mix into wide, shallow bowls. Top each bowl with three asparagus spears, then the fish.

chicken, poultry

Crisp-skin chicken, parsnip mash, roasted asparagus and salsa verde
Duck pastie, wilted greens, apple and currant chutney
Slow-cooked duck, red cabbage, bacon and hazelnuts
Moroccan chicken, kalamata olives, preserved lemon and coriander
Quail wrapped in coppa with ricotta and sage
Roast young chicken with paprika, cumin and garlic
Spatchcock with couscous, yoghurt and butter beans
Garlic chicken with salad of spinach, nashi, goat's cheese and dukkah
Slow-cooked duck, polenta, pancetta and ruby chard
Grilled quail, tuscan bean stew and crisp pancetta
Young chicken with pancetta, broad beans, beet leaves and herbed mascarpone

Crisp-skin chicken, parsnip mash, roasted asparagus and salsa verde

Serves 6 as a main course

jus (Basics page 175)

1/2 cup (125ml/4 1/2 fl oz) salsa verde (Basics page 168)

parsnip mash (Side Dishes page 121)

3 x 1.1kg (2 lb 7 oz) chickens, boned breast with wing attached and thigh boned, or 6 x No. 16 kiev cut chicken breasts, skin on

salt/pepper

extra-virgin olive oil

2 bunches (400g/13 oz) young asparagus, woody ends removed

knob of unsalted butter

Prepare jus, salsa verde and parsnip mash as recipes direct.

Preheat oven to 220°C (425°F/Gas 7). Heat an oven tray in oven until hot. Season chicken with salt and black pepper. Heat a wide, heavy-based pan over very high heat, add a little olive oil, then place chicken, skin side down, in pan. When well-coloured, remove from pan and place chicken, skin side up on the hot oven tray and roast for 8-10 minutes. Skin may be further crisped if desired by placing under a hot grill. Remove from oven and allow chicken to rest for 5 minutes.

Halve asparagus spears diagonally. Heat a heavy-based ovenproof pan over very high heat, add a little olive oil, the asparagus, then season with salt and black pepper. Sauté briefly, add the knob of butter and place pan in the oven for several minutes until asparagus is tender.

To serve, place a large spoonful of hot parsnip mash onto the centre of each plate. Place chicken alongside. Accompany with asparagus and a spoonful of salsa verde. Drizzle a little hot jus over chicken.

See photograph page 91

Roast ducks are available from Chinatown or you could use our recipe for slow-cooked duck (Basics page 177). The Chinese-style ducks are cooked with Asian spices so you may like to substitute shiitake mushrooms for the field mushrooms. If you prefer not to make your own puff pastry, use a good quality butter puff pastry from a patisserie.

Duck pastie, wilted greens, apple and currant chutney

Serves 6 as a main course

500ml (18 fl oz) jus (Basics page 175)
2 roasted ducks or 6 slow-cooked duck thigh-and-leg portions (Basics page 177)
apple and currant chutney (Basics page 174)
olive oil, for cooking
3 shallots (french shallots), sliced
2 cloves garlic, crushed
150g (5 oz) field (open-flat or swiss brown) mushrooms, wiped and thinly sliced
1 teaspoon thyme leaves
salt/pepper
6 x 16cm (6½ in) diameter puff pastry rounds
1 egg, beaten lightly, for egg wash
2 tablespoons sesame seed
wilted greens (Side Dishes page 121)

Prepare jus, duck and apple and currant chutney as recipes direct.

Heat a little olive oil in a heavy-based pan and sauté shallots and garlic until shallots are transparent. Add mushrooms and thyme and continue to cook until no juices remain. Add 1 cup (250ml/9 fl oz) jus, bring to the boil and cook until sauce is of a syrupy consistency. Taste and season with salt and black pepper. Remove from heat and allow to cool.

Remove flesh from duck and discard bones, fat and excess skin. Cut duck meat into large dice. Add enough cooled sauce to duck meat to thoroughly moisten.

Preheat oven to 220°C (425°F/Gas 7). Brush puff pastry rounds with egg wash, then divide filling between them. Draw pastry up to a crescent at centre top and crimp edges together to seal. Brush pasties with egg wash and sprinkle with sesame seed. Place on an oven tray lined with baking (silicone) paper and bake 15-20 minutes or until golden.

Meanwhile, prepare wilted greens as recipe directs.

To serve, centre a pastie on each plate and place wilted greens to one side. Accompany with chutney and drizzle a little hot jus over and around the pastie.

Slow-cooked duck, red cabbage, bacon and hazelnuts

Serves 4 as a main course

4 slow-cooked duck thigh-and-leg portions (Basics page 177)

jus (Basics page 175)

red cabbage with bacon and hazelnuts (Side Dishes page 124)

Prepare slow-cooked duck and jus as recipes direct.

Preheat oven to 180°C (350°F/Gas 4). Remove duck from fat, place on an oven tray and warm through in the oven. Preheat grill to hot and grill duck to further crisp the skin.

Meanwhile, prepare red cabbage with bacon and hazelnuts as recipe directs.

To serve, place warm cabbage on serving plates, add bacon and hazelnuts, then top with a crisped duck portion and spoon over some hot jus.

Right: Slow-cooked duck, red cabbage, bacon and hazelnuts (recipe this page)

Top: Slow cooked duck, grilled polenta, pancetta and ruby chard (recipe page 98)

Above: Spatchcock with couscous, yoghurt and butter beans (recipe page 96)

Right: Crisp-skin chicken, parsnip mash, roasted asparagus and salsa verde (recipe page 86)

The sauce for this dish can be prepared in advance. Add the olives and lemon when reheating, then fold through the coriander just before serving. Serve with steamed couscous (see Side Dishes page 122) or rice.

Moroccan chicken, kalamata olives, preserved lemon and coriander

Serves 6 as a main course

½ salted lemon, flesh discarded, skin shredded (Basics page 173)

600ml (21 fl oz) rich tomato sauce (Basics page 171)

2 roasted red peppers (capsicum), peeled and cut into thick strips (Basics page 164)

3 x 1.1kg (2 lb 7 oz) chickens, boned breast with wing attached and thigh boned or 6 x No.16 kiev cut chicken breasts, skin removed

olive oil, for cooking

1 red onion, sliced

2 cloves garlic, crushed

1½ cups (225g/8 oz) polenta (yellow cornmeal), for dusting

1 cup (155g/5 oz) kalamata olives, pitted

½ cup coriander leaves

½ cup (125ml/4 fl oz) greek-style natural yoghurt

coriander leaves

marinade

½ teaspoon dried chilli flakes

1 teaspoon spanish paprika (preferably La Chinata bittersweet paprika)

2 cloves garlic, crushed

I lemon, grated zest of whole, juice of half

½ cup (125ml/4½ fl oz) extra-virgin olive oil

Prepare salted lemon, rich tomato sauce and roasted peppers as recipes direct.

To make the marinade, whisk together chilli flakes, paprika, garlic, lemon zest and juice and the extra-virgin olive oil until blended. Pour over chicken portions and allow to marinate in the refrigerator at least several hours or overnight.

Heat a heavy-based saucepan over moderate heat, add a little olive oil and sweat onion and garlic until onion is transparent. Add roasted peppers and rich tomato sauce to pan, adjust seasonings and bring to the boil. Remove from heat and keep warm.

Preheat oven to 200°C (400°F/Gas 6). Heat an oven tray in oven until hot. Pour polenta into a shallow tray. Remove chicken from marinade and coat both sides with polenta. Heat a wide, heavy-based pan over moderate heat, add a little olive oil, then cook chicken breasts until golden on both sides, adding more oil if required. Place chicken in a single layer on the hot oven tray and roast for 8-10 minutes. Remove from oven and allow to rest for several minutes.

Just prior to serving, fold olives, salted lemon and coriander leaves into hot sauce. Divide sauce between serving plates. Top each with a chicken breast and finish with a spoonful of yoghurt. Scatter with additional coriander leaves.

Left: Eye fillet, wet polenta, garlic confit and radicchio (recipe page 104)

The spiced chickpeas may be served at room temperature or reheated if preferred.

Quail wrapped in coppa with ricotta and sage

Serves 6 as a main course

jus (Basics page 175)

6 long, thin slices coppa (see Glossary) or substitute prosciutto

sage leaves

120g (4 oz) ricotta

6 medium quail, opened-out and boned

olive oil, for cooking

250g (9 oz) young ruby chard (red swiss chard), stems removed

spiced chickpeas

3 cups cooked or canned, drained chickpeas

extra-virgin olive oil

1 onion, diced

1 large carrot, diced

1 stick celery, diced

1 small leek, sliced and well washed

2 cloves garlic, crushed

pinch dried chilli flakes

400g (13 oz) can roma (italian plum) tomatoes, chopped, with juice

1½ teaspoons cumin seed, roasted and ground

¼ cup oregano leaves

1 lemon, juice only

salt/pepper

Prepare jus as recipe directs. If you prefer to cook your own chickpeas, refer to method (Basics page 164).

To finish the chickpeas, heat a little extra-virgin olive oil in a heavy-based saucepan over moderate heat and gently cook the onion, carrot, celery, leek, garlic and chilli flakes until onion is soft. Add tomatoes, cooked chickpeas and ground cumin, simmer for 15 minutes. Remove from heat, add oregano leaves and lemon juice, season with salt and black pepper.

Lay coppa flat on a cutting board, top each slice with three sage leaves. Place 1 tablespoon of the ricotta under the skin of each quail and lay bird on coppa, skin side down. Wrap quail in coppa, with join on the underside.

Preheat oven to 220°C (425°F/Gas 7). Heat a heavy-based, ovenproof frying pan over high heat and brush lightly with olive oil. Place birds, skin side up, in pan and sear on the underside. Turn birds over and place pan in oven to roast for 5 minutes. Remove from oven and allow to rest for 5 minutes.

Place chard in a hot pan with a little olive oil season and cook, stirring, until just wilted.

To serve, place a spoonful of the spiced chickpeas on each plate and rest quail on top. Arrange some wilted chard next to quail and drizzle with jus. Pour a little extra-virgin olive oil over the chickpeas.

At the restaurant we use a boned thigh and a breast from a good quality No.11 or 1.1kg (2 lb 4 oz) chicken. The Spanish paprika we use is La Chinata bittersweet, which has a distinctive smoky taste and bears no resemblance to mass-produced supermarket quality paprikas.

Roast young chicken with paprika, cumin and garlic

Serves 6 as a main course

6 x 160g (5 oz) chicken breasts, skin on, boned
panzanella (Side Dishes page 122)
salt/pepper
3 limes, halved

marinade

$1\frac{1}{2}$ teaspoons spanish paprika
$1\frac{1}{2}$ teaspoons cumin seed, roasted and ground
pinch dried chilli flakes
l lemon, grated zest and juice
2 cloves garlic, crushed
$\frac{1}{2}$ cup (125ml/$4\frac{1}{2}$ fl oz) olive oil

For the marinade, combine paprika, ground cumin, chilli flakes, lemon zest and juice, garlic and olive oil in a shallow dish. Lay chicken in a single layer in marinade so the skin is above the liquid – this will give a crisper skin when cooking. Allow to marinate for 24 hours, refrigerated.

Prepare panzanella as recipe directs.

Preheat oven to 220°C (425°F/Gas 7). Heat an oven tray in oven until hot. Remove chicken from marinade and season with salt and black pepper. Heat a wide, heavy-based pan over high heat with a little olive oil. Add chicken to pan, skin side down, and allow to colour well. Turn chicken and place on the hot oven tray to roast for 10 minutes or until breast is cooked but still moist. Remove from oven and allow to rest for 5 minutes.

To serve, place a large spoonful of panzanella on each plate, top with a chicken breast, skin side up, and accompany with half a lime.

To marinate the birds, use the marinade from the recipe for roast young chicken with paprika, cumin and garlic.

Spatchcock with couscous, yoghurt and butter beans

Serves 6 as a main course

marinade (see roast young chicken with paprika, cumin and garlic page 95)

6 x spatchcocks, opened-out and boned with leg bones remaining

couscous (Side Dishes page 122)

500g (17 oz) butter beans, stalks removed, left whole

1/2 cup (125ml/4 1/2 fl oz) greek-style natural yoghurt

3 limes, halved

Combine marinade ingredients in a shallow dish. Lay spatchcocks in a single layer in marinade so the skin is above the liquid – this will give a crisper skin when roasting. Allow to marinate in refrigerator for several hours or overnight.

Prepare couscous as recipe directs.

Preheat grill to moderately hot. Remove spatchcocks from marinade. Brush skin with some of the marinade just prior to placing birds under the grill, and grill until golden. Turn birds and cook the second side. Remove chicken from grill and allow to rest for 5 minutes.

Meanwhile, bring a small saucepan of salted water to the boil and blanch butter beans until just tender. Drain well.

To serve, place a large spoonful of couscous on each plate with a spatchcock to one side. Add butter beans topped with a dollop of yoghurt and serve with half a lime.

See photograph page 90

Dukkah can be made up to two weeks in advance and kept in an airtight container. If required it can be refreshed in a 180°C (350°F/Gas 4) oven until fragrant. Use leftover dukkah as a dip. Slice crusty bread, dip into extra-virgin olive oil then into the dukkah.

Garlic chicken with salad of spinach, nashi, goat's cheese and dukkah

Serves 6 as a main course

jus (Basics page 175)
2 cups flat-leaf parsley
1 head garlic confit (Basics page 167)
3 x 1.1kg (2 lb 7 oz) chickens, boned breast with wing attached and thigh boned or 6 x No.16 kiev cut chicken breasts, skin on
olive oil, for cooking
salt/pepper

dukkah

3/4 cup (120g/4 oz) hazelnuts, roasted and skinned
1/3 cup (50g/2 oz) sesame seed
1/4 cup (25g/1 oz) coriander seed
2 tablespoons (20g/1 oz) cumin seed
salt/pepper, to taste

salad

200g (7 oz) baby english spinach leaves, stems removed
1/2 red onion, finely diced
2 nashi pears, quartered, cored and thinly sliced
200g (7 oz) fresh goat's cheese, crumbled
extra-virgin olive oil

Prepare jus as recipe directs.

To make dukkah, combine all ingredients in a blender (or use a mortar and pestle) and grind or crush to a semi-coarse texture. Place mixture in a little hot olive oil in a non-stick frying pan and roast over moderate heat, stirring occasionally, until aromatic. Cool and store in an airtight container.

Preheat oven to 220°C (425°F/Gas 7). Heat an oven tray in oven until hot. Place parsley and garlic in a blender (or use a mortar and pestle) and mix to a paste. Spread 2 teaspoons of paste as evenly as possible under the skin of each chicken portion.

Heat a wide, heavy-based pan over very high heat, add a little olive oil. Season chicken with salt and black pepper, then place chicken, skin side down, in pan and seal. Turn chicken and place on the hot oven tray and roast for 8-10 minutes. Remove from oven and allow to rest for 5 minutes.

For the salad, combine spinach, onion, nashi and goat's cheese in a large bowl. Dress with a little extra-virgin olive oil and toss lightly.

To serve, if required, place chicken briefly under hot grill to heat through before serving. Place a chicken portion on each plate. Divide salad between plates next to chicken. Sprinkle dukkah over salad. Pour a little hot jus over and around the chicken.

Slow-cooked duck, polenta, pancetta and ruby chard

Serves 4 as a main course

jus (Basics page 175)
4 slow-cooked duck thigh-and-leg portions (Basics page 177)
8 slices pancetta
wet polenta (Side Dishes page 123)
extra-virgin olive oil
150g (5 oz) young ruby chard (red swiss chard), stems removed
salt/pepper

Prepare jus and slow-cooked duck as recipes direct.

Preheat oven to 180°C (350°F/Gas 4). Remove duck from fat, place on an oven tray and warm through in the oven. Preheat grill to hot and grill duck to further crisp the skin. Place pancetta on an oven tray and grill until crisp.

Meanwhile, prepare wet polenta as recipe directs. Heat a heavy-based pan over high heat. Add a little extra-virgin olive oil and the chard. Season with salt and black pepper and toss to wilt.

To serve, place a spoonful of wet polenta on each plate, place crisp duck portion alongside. Top polenta with two slices grilled pancetta, sit wilted chard next to polenta and spoon a little hot jus over duck.

See photograph page 90

When in season, use fresh borlotti beans, or if time is short, use canned borlottis that have been well rinsed.

Grilled quail, tuscan bean stew and crisp pancetta

Serves 6 as a main course

tuscan bean stew (Side Dishes page 124)
6 quail, opened-out and boned
olive oil, for cooking
salt/pepper
1/2 cup basil leaves
12 slices pancetta, grilled or roasted until crisp

Prepare tuscan bean stew as recipe directs.

Preheat grill (or use a barbecue) to hot. Brush quail with olive oil and season with salt and black pepper. Cook quail under grill (or on the barbecue), ensuring you achieve good colour on the skin.

To serve, reheat tuscan bean stew, then fold in torn basil. Divide beans between wide, shallow bowls. Top with a quail and crisp pancetta.

Young chicken with pancetta, broad beans, beet leaves and herbed mascarpone

Serves 6 as a main course

jus (Basics page 175)

3 x 1.1kg (2 lb 7 oz) chickens, boned breast with wing attached and thigh boned or 6 x No.16 kiev cut chicken breasts, skin on

1 tablespoon each parsley, chives, basil and oregano, chopped

1 lemon, grated zest of whole, juice of half

300g (10 oz) mascarpone

12 thin slices pancetta

600g (1 lb 5 oz) podded broad beans

extra-virgin olive oil

150g (5 oz) baby beetroot leaves (or use ruby chard (red swiss chard))

salt/pepper

marinade

½ cup (125ml/4½ fl oz) olive oil

1 lemon, grated zest and juice

2 cloves garlic, crushed

2 teaspoons thyme leaves, chopped

Prepare jus as recipe directs.

For the marinade, combine olive oil, lemon zest and juice, garlic and thyme in a shallow dish. Immerse chicken in a single layer in marinade, skin side up, so skin remains uncovered by marinade – this gives a crisper skin when cooking. Allow to marinate at least 6 hours or overnight, refrigerated.

Using a wooden spoon, beat herbs, lemon zest and juice into mascarpone.

Preheat oven to 220°C (425°F/Gas 7). Heat an oven tray in oven until hot. Heat a wide, heavy-based pan over high heat. Wipe marinade from chicken and place, skin side down, in hot pan and sear until golden. Turn chicken and place on the hot oven tray to roast for 10 minutes or until chicken is cooked. Remove from oven and allow to rest for 5 minutes. Lay pancetta on tray and cook in oven until crisp.

Meanwhile, bring a small saucepan of salted water to the boil and cook broad beans until just tender. Drain. In a heavy-based saucepan, heat 1 tablespoon olive oil, add beet leaves and toss until just wilted. Add broad beans to leaves and season with salt and black pepper.

To serve, place a large spoonful of beet leaves and beans on each plate. Lay a chicken portion alongside with a dollop of herbed mascarpone. Top chicken with crisp pancetta and drizzle with hot jus.

meat

Braised veal shank with olives, thyme and lemon polenta
Eye fillet with quince jam, taleggio and rosemary potatoes
Eye fillet, wet polenta, garlic confit and radicchio
Fillet of beef with parsnips, baby leeks, tapenade and truffle oil
Lamb rump with salad of eggplant, salted lemon, chilli and watercress
Lamb loin, roast peppers, chickpeas and swiss chard
Double lamb cutlets, grilled red onion, eggplant and tabbouli
Roast lamb, caponata and balsamic potatoes
Lamb rack, farmhouse potatoes, mint and lemon
Pork with kipflers, sage, pancetta and spinach
Pork cutlets with parmesan potatoes, braised witlof and grilled apple

Braised veal shank with olives, thyme and lemon polenta

Serves 6 as a main course

Braised veal shanks (Basics page 178)
olive oil, for cooking
1 stick celery, diced
1 carrot, diced
1 leek, halved lengthwise, diced and well washed
2 cloves garlic, crushed
1 teaspoon thyme leaves, chopped
1 cup (150g/5 oz) kalamata olives, pitted
wet polenta (Side Dishes page 123)
1 tablespoon thyme leaves, chopped
2 lemons, grated zest only

Prepare braised veal shanks as recipe directs, except cool and store shanks on the bones in unreduced cooking liquor. When ready, remove shanks from stock then bring stock to the boil and reduce by half.

Heat a little olive oil in a large, heavy-based saucepan over moderate to high heat and sauté celery, carrot, leek, garlic and 1 teaspoon thyme until vegetables achieve some colour. Add reduced veal stock to vegetables and bring to the boil. Lower heat and allow mixture to reduce to a rich, glossy sauce, skimming occasionally. Add shanks to pan with the olives and heat through.

Meanwhile, prepare polenta as recipe directs and when cooked, fold through the tablespoon of thyme leaves and lemon zest.

To serve, place a large spoonful of lemon polenta on each wide shallow bowl, just off centre. Lay a warmed shank next to polenta, then spoon over a generous quantity of the sauce.

Taleggio is a soft, pungent cheese from Lombardy in Italy's north. Do not be put off by the strong smell of this cheese, the flavour, by comparison, is mild. A crisp green salad with balsamic dressing (Basics page 171) would be a good accompaniment for this dish.

Eye fillet with quince jam, taleggio and rosemary potatoes

Serves 6 as a main course

jus (Basics page 175)
rosemary potatoes (see oven-roasted potatoes, Side Dishes page 125)
6 x 200g (7 oz) eye fillet of beef, centre-cut
extra-virgin olive oil
salt/pepper
180g (6 oz) taleggio, sliced into six pieces
3 tablespoons quince jam (preferably Maggie Beer's quince paste)

Prepare jus and rosemary potatoes as recipes direct.

Meanwhile, preheat oven to 250°C (500°F/Gas 9). Heat a wide, heavy-based ovenproof frying pan over very high heat. Brush steaks with olive oil on both sides and season with salt and black pepper. Sear steaks on one side until a good colour is achieved, turn meat, place pan in oven and roast 8-10 minutes or until medium-rare. Remove from oven and allow meat to rest for 5 minutes.

To serve, divide potatoes between serving plates and top with a slice of taleggio. Place steak alongside. Spoon a little quince jam onto each plate. Drizzle hot jus over and around steak.

A variation on this recipe would be to serve the fillet of beef and wet polenta with gorgonzola folded through the polenta, with wilted swiss chard (silverbeet) and onion jam (Basics page 173).

Eye fillet, wet polenta, garlic confit and radicchio

Serves 6 as a main course

6 heads garlic confit (Basics page 167)
jus (Basics page 175)
wet polenta (Side Dishes page 123)
radicchio and bacon (Side Dishes page 127)
6 x 200g (7 oz) eye fillet of beef, centre-cut
extra-virgin olive oil
salt/pepper

Prepare garlic confit, jus, wet polenta and bacon and radicchio (omitting bacon) as recipes direct.

Meanwhile, preheat oven to 250°C (500°F/Gas 9). Heat a wide, heavy-based ovenproof frying pan over very high heat. Brush steaks with olive oil on both sides and season with salt and black pepper. Sear steaks on one side until good colour is achieved, turn meat, place pan in oven and roast 8-10 minutes or until medium-rare. Remove from oven and allow meat to rest for 5 minutes.

To serve, place a large spoonful of wet polenta on each plate. Place a steak and some radicchio alongside. Sit a head of garlic confit between steak and polenta and drizzle hot jus over and around.

See photograph page 92

Baby leeks are similar in appearance to large green (spring) onions, but the leaves of the leek are flatter and darker. To prepare baby leeks, cut off the root ends, then remove the darker outer leaves before rinsing well to remove all grit.

Fillet of beef with parsnips, baby leeks, tapenade and truffle oil

Serves 6 as a main course

tapenade (Basics page 166)
jus (Basics page 175)
6 medium parsnips, peeled
few sprigs thyme
5 cloves garlic, unpeeled, lightly crushed
olive oil, for cooking
500ml (18 fl oz) chicken stock (Basics page 176)
24 baby leeks, trimmed and cleaned
6 x 200g (7 oz) eye fillet of beef, centre-cut
salt/pepper
18 medium asparagus spears, woody ends removed
1 tablespoon unsalted butter
truffle oil (see Glossary)

Prepare tapenade and jus as recipes direct.

Preheat oven to 180°C (350°F/Gas 4). Halve parsnips lengthwise and remove cores. In a bowl, combine thyme, garlic and a little olive oil with parsnips. Mix well to coat then place parsnips on oven tray and roast until tender.

Bring chicken stock to the boil in a wide, shallow pan, add whole leeks then reduce heat and simmer until tender.

Increase oven temperature to 250°C (500°F/Gas 9). Heat a wide, heavy-based ovenproof frying pan over very high heat. Brush steaks with olive oil on both sides and season with salt and black pepper. Sear steaks on one side until good colour is achieved, turn meat and place pan in oven and roast 8-10 minutes or until medium-rare. Remove from oven and allow meat to rest for 5 minutes.

Meanwhile, halve asparagus diagonally and blanch in a saucepan of boiling salted water. Drain, then toss asparagus in a bowl with butter, salt and black pepper.

To serve, place steak just off-centre on plate, place parsnips, leeks and asparagus alongside. Drizzle vegetables with a little truffle oil. Spoon a little tapenade onto leeks. Pour hot jus over steak.

Lamb rump is best cooked medium (pink). When only cooked to rare or medium-rare, the sinew that runs through the centre of the rump remains uncooked and visible.

Lamb rump with salad of eggplant, salted lemon, chilli and watercress

Serves 6 as a main course

2 teaspoons chopped salted lemon skin (Basics page 173)

jus (Basics page 175)

2 small eggplant (aubergine), sliced 1.5cm (3/4 in) thick

olive oil, for cooking

6 x 200g (7 oz) lamb rumps, trimmed, leaving a little fat

salt/pepper

red wine vinaigrette (Basics page 171)

120g (4 oz) watercress

1 cup coriander leaves

1 red chilli, seeded and sliced diagonally

1 red onion, thinly sliced into rings

Prepare salted lemons and jus as recipes direct.

Preheat grill (or barbecue) to high. Brush eggplant slices with a little olive oil and grill (or barbecue) until tender and well-coloured. Keep warm.

Preheat oven to 230°C (450°F/Gas 7-8). Heat an oven tray in oven until hot. Heat a wide, heavy-based frying pan over high heat. Brush lamb with olive oil and season with salt and black pepper. Seal lamb in pan achieving good colour on all sides. Place lamb on the hot oven tray and roast approximately 15 minutes or until medium. Remove from oven and allow to rest for 5 minutes.

Meanwhile, prepare red wine vinaigrette as recipe directs. Combine warm eggplant slices, watercress, coriander, chilli, onion and salted lemon in a bowl and dress lightly with enough of the vinaigrette to moisten.

To serve, divide salad between large, shallow serving bowls. Carve lamb rumps into four or five slices and arrange on top of salad. Drizzle over a little hot jus.

Lamb loin, roast peppers, chickpeas and swiss chard

Serves 6 as a main course

400g (13 oz) cooked chickpeas (Basics page 164)

600ml (21 fl oz) rich tomato sauce (Basics page 171)

3 roasted red peppers (capsicum), peeled and thickly sliced (Basics page 164)

jus (Basics page 175)

roasted garlic mayonnaise (Basics page 167)

2 tablespoons extra-virgin olive oil

2 red onions, diced

2 cloves garlic, crushed

1 carrot, diced (to size of chickpeas)

1 red chilli, seeded and finely chopped

2 teaspoons cumin seed, roasted and ground

lemon juice, to taste

salt/pepper

½ cup flat-leaf parsley, chopped

6 x 200g (7 oz) lamb loins, denuded (silver skin removed)

150g (5 oz) young swiss chard (silverbeet), stems removed

Prepare chickpeas, rich tomato sauce, roasted peppers, jus and roasted garlic mayonnaise as recipes direct.

Heat a heavy-based pan over moderate heat, add olive oil and sweat the onions, garlic, carrot and chilli until carrot is tender. Add cooked chickpeas, cumin and rich tomato sauce. Season with lemon juice, salt and black pepper to taste. Toss through parsley just prior to serving.

Preheat oven to 230°C (450°F/Gas 7-8), place an oven tray in oven until hot. Heat a wide, heavy-based frying pan over high heat until very hot. Brush lamb loins with olive oil, season with salt and black pepper and sear in pan on both sides. Place on the hot oven tray and roast for 8-10 minutes until medium (pink). Remove from oven and allow to rest for 5 minutes before slicing.

Meanwhile, warm the peppers in oven and keep warm. Heat a clean pan over high heat, add a little olive oil then chard, season with salt and black pepper. Toss until just wilted.

To serve, place a large spoonful of warm chickpea mixture in centre of serving plates, top with peppers and chard. Carve each lamb loin diagonally into three slices and arrange on top of chickpeas. Drizzle a little hot jus over lamb and top with a spoonful of roasted garlic mayonnaise.

Lamb should be marinated overnight or at least several hours for best results.

Double lamb cutlets, grilled red onion, eggplant and tabbouli

Serves 6 as a main course

jus (Basics page 175)
tabbouli (Side Dishes page 126)
3 x 8-cutlet lamb racks, best end
6 x 2cm (3/4 in) thick slices eggplant (aubergine)
salt/pepper
4 red onions
1 tablespoon unsalted butter
2 tablespoons red wine vinegar (see Glossary)

marinade

1 teaspoon cumin seed, roasted and ground
1 teaspoon coriander seed, roasted and ground
l lemon, grated zest only
1 clove garlic, crushed
1/2 cup (125ml/4 1/2 fl oz) olive oil

Prepare jus and tabbouli as recipes direct.

Cut racks into two-cutlet sections. Remove the bone nearest the edge of each pair, leaving meat on either side of one bone, giving you twelve double lamb cutlets. For the marinade, combine ground cumin and coriander, lemon zest, garlic and olive oil. Brush liberally over lamb and allow to marinate, refrigerated.

Brush eggplant slices on both sides with a little olive oil, season with salt and black pepper and char-grill using a ridged grill pan until tender and well-coloured (or use a grill or barbecue) .

Cut onions into wedges, leaving root end intact to hold segments together. Heat a heavy-based frying pan over high heat, add a little olive oil and the onion wedges, season with salt and black pepper and cook until onions begin to colour. Add butter, reduce heat to moderate and cook until onions are tender and have softened. Add vinegar, remove pan from heat, cover and allow flavours to infuse.

Preheat oven to 230°C (450°F/Gas 7-8). Heat an oven tray in oven until hot. Heat a wide, heavy-based pan over high heat and sear meat on all sides. Place lamb on the hot oven tray and roast for 8-10 minutes or until medium (pink).

To serve, place two heaped tablespoons of tabbouli off-centre on each plate. Lay one slice of eggplant alongside. Add some onion wedges and place two cutlets on top. Drizzle hot jus over and around cutlets.

Right: Double lamb cutlets, grilled red onion, eggplant and tabbouli (recipe this page)

Above: Pork cutlets with parmesan potatoes, braised witlof and grilled apple (recipe page 116)

Top Right: Roasted southern golds, chorizo, chilli and coriander (recipe page 125)

Right: Green beans with mustard cream (recipe page 127)

Roast lamb, caponata and balsamic potatoes

Serves 6 as a main course

caponata (Side Dishes page 126)
jus (Basics page 175)
1.5kg ($3^1/_2$ lb) leg of lamb
extra-virgin olive oil
salt/pepper
3 sprigs rosemary
balsamic potatoes (see oven-roasted potatoes, Side Dishes page 125)

Prepare caponata and jus as recipes direct.

Preheat oven to 180°C (350°F/Gas 4). Place lamb in a roasting pan, brush with olive oil and season with salt and black pepper. Scatter with rosemary and roast for 60-80 minutes – juices will run pink when meat is pierced. Remove lamb from oven and allow to rest for 10 minutes before slicing.

Meanwhile, prepare balsamic potatoes as recipe directs.

To serve, place a large spoonful of warm caponata just off centre of serving plates. Slice leg of lamb and arrange alongside. Divide balsamic potatoes between plates and drizzle hot jus over lamb.

Top right: Radicchio and bacon (recipe page 127)

Right: Salad of avocado lime, coriander and almonds (recipe page 118)

Lamb rack, farmhouse potatoes, mint and lemon

Serves 6 as a main course

2 salted lemons (Basics page 173)
1 cup (250ml/9 fl oz) jus (Basics page 175)
1 cup (250ml/9 fl oz) extra-virgin olive oil
2 tablespoons sugar
1 cup mint
1 cup green (spring) onions, thinly sliced diagonally
6 x 300g (10 oz) 4-cutlet lamb racks
farmhouse potatoes (see oven-roasted potatoes, Side Dishes page 125)
250g (9 oz) young swiss chard (silverbeet), stems removed
salt/pepper

Prepare salted lemons and jus as recipes direct.

Whisk together olive oil and sugar, stir in mint and onions. Discard flesh from salted lemons, rinse the skin, finely dice, add to mixture and set aside.

Preheat oven to 230°C (450°F/Gas 7-8). Heat an oven tray in oven until hot. Brush lamb with a little extra olive oil, season with salt and pepper. Heat a wide, heavy-based pan over very high heat, add lamb racks and sear on all sides. Place lamb on the hot oven tray and roast 15-20 minutes until medium (pink). Remove from oven and allow to rest for 10 minutes.

Meanwhile, prepare farmhouse potatoes as recipe directs. Heat a clean pan over high heat, add a little olive oil then chard, season with salt and black pepper. Toss until just wilted.

To serve, divide potatoes between plates with chard to one side. Halve lamb racks and arrange on plates. Pour hot jus over and around lamb. Accompany with mint and lemon mix.

High quality pork is one of the most difficult meats to source. We use suckling pork from Gungel Farm near Tenterfield, New South Wales but although this product is excellent, it is not widely available. Duck fat gives these potatoes great flavour, however if none is available, use a good extra-virgin olive oil. The elongated kipfler potato has yellow, waxy flesh and is ideal for baking.

Pork with kipflers, sage, pancetta and spinach

Serves 6 as a main course

jus (Basics page 175)

olive oil, for cooking

6 x 200g (7 oz) pork loin portions, skin removed, some fat remaining or 6 x 180g (6 oz) pork fillets, denuded (fat and sinew removed)

salt/pepper

18 kipfler potatoes, unpeeled

125 g (4½ oz) duck fat (or use olive oil)

½ cup sage leaves

12 thin slices pancetta

440g (15 oz) english spinach leaves, stems removed

Prepare jus as recipe directs.

Preheat oven to 220°C (425°F/Gas 7). Heat an oven tray in oven until hot. Heat a heavy-based pan over high heat and add a little olive oil. Season pork portions with salt and black pepper and sear on all sides. Place, skin side down, on the hot oven tray and roast 15-20 minutes. Remove from oven and allow pork to rest for 5-8 minutes. (If using fillets, cook using same method and roast approximately 10-12 minutes).

Meanwhile, cut each potato lengthwise into three slices and dry on absorbent paper. Place on an oven tray lined with baking (silicone) paper, brush liberally with duck fat and season with salt and black pepper. Place potatoes in the oven and roast until tender and well-coloured. Stir through sage leaves, roast a further 5 minutes. Remove pan from oven, grill pancetta until crisp, then add to potatoes and keep warm.

Heat a heavy-based frying pan over high heat and add a little olive oil. Add spinach, season with salt and pepper and toss until just wilted.

To serve, place potato, sage and pancetta mixture on plate. Slice pork thinly and arrange on edge of potatoes. Divide spinach between plates and pour hot jus over and around pork.

Pork cutlets with parmesan potatoes, braised witlof and grilled apple

Serves 6 as a main course

jus (Basics page 175)
clarified butter (Basics page 164)
6 medium witlof (belgian endive), halved lengthwise
1 teaspoon caraway seed, roasted and ground
salt/pepper
300ml (11 fl oz) orange juice, freshly squeezed
2 teaspoons unsalted butter
1/4 cup flat-leaf parsley, shredded
parmesan potatoes (see oven-roasted potatoes, Side Dishes page 125)
extra-virgin olive oil
12 pork cutlets
3 granny smith apples, peeled, cored and thickly sliced

Prepare jus as recipe directs.

Heat oven to 190°C (Gas 5). Heat a heavy-based ovenproof pan (or use a flameproof casserole) over high heat. Add 2 tablespoons clarified butter, witlof and caraway seed, season with salt and black pepper and sauté briefly until witlof are lightly coloured. Add orange juice and bring to the boil. Cover and bake for 10-15 minutes or until witlof are tender. Using a slotted spoon, remove witlof from pan, then reduce sauce until thick and glossy. Whisk in 2 teaspoons butter, then return witlof to pan and keep warm. Fold through parsley, just prior to serving.

Meanwhile, prepare parmesan potatoes as recipe directs.

Increase oven temperature to 220°C (42°F/Gas 7). Heat an oven tray in oven until hot. Heat a wide, heavy-based frying pan over high heat and add a little olive oil. Season pork cutlets with salt and black pepper and seal on both sides. Place on the hot oven tray and roast for 10-15 minutes. Remove from oven and allow pork to rest for 5 minutes.

Brush apple slices with a little extra clarified butter and grill or pan-fry until tender.

To serve, place two cutlets on each plate with several slices of the parmesan potatoes. Place two witlof halves next to potatoes and spoon some of the reduced orange sauce over. Top cutlets with grilled apple and spoon hot jus over pork.

See photograph page 110

side dishes

Spiced avocado
Salad of avocado, lime, coriander and almonds
Salad of witlof, rocket, gorgonzola and crisp bacon
Shaved baby fennel, grain mustard and lemon
Chilli Corncakes
Champ
Slow-cooked fennel
Parsnip mash
Wilted greens
Panzanella
Couscous
Polenta – wet/grilled
Tuscan bean stew
Red cabbage with bacon and hazelnuts
Oven-roasted potatoes
Roasted southern golds, chorizo, chilli and coriander
Caponata
Tabbouli
Radicchio and bacon
Green beans with mustard cream
Pumpkin, chilli, coriander and hommus
Mushrooms, garlic, thyme and goat's cheese

Spiced avocado

Serves 6 as a side dish

½ lemon, juice only
½ lime, juice only
½ red onion, finely diced
½ cup coriander leaves
2 tablespoons mango chutney (preferably Sharwoods Green Label)
1 teaspoon sambal oelek (see Glossary)
pinch cumin seed, roasted and ground
extra-virgin olive oil
3 avocados, halved, stone removed and peeled
salt/pepper

Combine the citrus juices, onion, coriander leaves, chutney, sambal oelek and ground cumin in a bowl. Add a splash of extra-virgin olive oil then gently fold in diced avocado flesh. Season to taste with salt and black pepper.

Salad of avocado, lime, coriander and almonds

Serves 4

4 avocados, halved and stone removed
1 small red onion, thinly sliced into rings
½ cup (60g/2 oz) whole blanched almonds, roasted
2 limes, juice only
½ teaspoon cumin seed, roasted and ground
3 tablespoons coriander leaves
extra-virgin olive oil
salt/pepper

Using a very large spoon, slide it between avocado flesh and skin and scoop out avocado half. Dice flesh into large pieces and place in a large mixing bowl. Add onion, almonds, lime juice, ground cumin and coriander leaves and mix gently with enough of the olive oil to moisten. Season with salt and black pepper, then place in a serving dish.

See photograph page 112

Salad of witlof, rocket, gorgonzola and crisp bacon

Serves 4

150g (5 oz) italian gorgonzola, fully matured
3 witlof (belgian endive), leaves separated
250g (9 oz) rocket leaves
12 thin rashers bacon, grilled until crisp
balsamic dressing (Basics page 171)

Thinly slice gorgonzola using a hot knife – it may crumble a little. Just before serving, combine witlof, rocket, gorgonzola and bacon in a large bowl and dress lightly with enough of the dressing to moisten. Arrange in a serving dish.

If baby fennel is unavailable, use mature fennel by first discarding roots and firmer or blemished outer leaves.

Shaved baby fennel, grain mustard and lemon

Serves 4

4 baby fennel bulbs, halved, shaved lengthwise
1 red onion, thinly sliced
2 tablespoons chives, chopped
2 lemons, juice only
1 tablespoon grain mustard (preferably Hill Farm Mountain Pepper)
extra-virgin olive oil
salt/pepper

Combine shaved fennel, onion and chives in a bowl. Add lemon juice and mustard and mix lightly, adding enough olive oil to moisten. Season with salt and black pepper and allow flavours to infuse for 30 minutes before serving.

Chilli corncakes

Makes 8

- 2 cobs sweet corn, husked
- olive oil
- 100g (3½ oz) plain flour
- 2 teaspoons baking powder
- ¼ teaspoon bicarbonate of soda
- salt/pepper
- 250ml (9 fl oz) buttermilk
- 2 eggs, separated
- 3 tablespoons mixed coriander leaves and flat-leaf parsley, chopped
- ½ teaspoon red chilli, finely chopped
- clarified butter (Basics 164)

Cut corn kernels from cobs and roast in a hot frying pan over high heat with a little oil until golden. Allow to cool.

Place flour in a mixing bowl, add baking powder and bicarbonate of soda and season with salt and black pepper. Combine buttermilk and egg yolks and whisk into flour mixture. Fold in roasted corn, herbs and chilli. Whisk egg whites to soft peaks and fold into batter.

Heat a blini pan (see Glossary) over moderate heat, brush with a little melted clarified butter and cook corncakes until bases are golden. Drizzle tops with a little clarified butter. Place pan under a preheated moderate grill and cook until golden. Allow to cool.

To serve, reheat in a moderate oven for 5-8 minutes or until just warm.

Truffle mash, a variation on champ, has long been an e'cco favourite. It goes well with grilled meats, poultry or seared salmon.

Champ

Serves 6

- 1.2kg (2 lb 10 oz) pink-skinned, waxy potatoes such as desiree, peeled and diced
- 250ml (9 fl oz) milk
- 125ml (4½ fl oz) cream
- 125g (4½ oz) unsalted butter
- 8 green (spring) onions, thinly sliced diagonally
- 2 tablespoons salted capers, well rinsed
- sea salt and ground white pepper

Boil potatoes in salted water until tender, drain then pass through a mouli or mash. Place milk, cream and butter in a saucepan, bring to the boil, then gradually stir into potatoes to achieve a light, smooth consistency. Fold in onions and capers. Season with salt and white pepper.

For Truffle Mash: Omit onions and capers. Stir through 1 tablespoon of truffle oil (see Glossary).

It is important to use baby fennel. If unavailable, separate a large bulb of fennel into leaves, halve diagonally and trim to shape by cutting on the diagonal.

Slow-cooked fennel

Serves 6

60ml (2 fl oz) olive oil
6 heads baby fennel, halved
4 cloves garlic, unpeeled and lightly crushed
400ml (13 fl oz) chicken stock (Basics page 176)

Heat olive oil in a saucepan, add the fennel and cook for several minutes. Add the garlic and cook until fennel colours slightly. Add chicken stock and bring to the boil. Reduce heat, cover and simmer until fennel is soft. Lift fennel from stock and serve, discard garlic.

Parsnip mash

Serves 6

8 medium pink-skinned waxy potatoes such as desiree, peeled and diced
8 parsnips, peeled, cored and diced
250ml (9 fl oz) milk
125ml (4½ fl oz) cream
125g (4½ oz) unsalted butter
sea salt and ground white pepper

Boil potatoes in salted water until tender, drain then pass through a mouli or mash. Steam parsnips until tender, pass through a mouli or sieve to purée. Heat milk, cream and butter to the boil, then gradually stir into potatoes to achieve a light, smooth consistency. Fold in parsnip purée. Taste and season with salt and white pepper.

Wilted greens

Serves 6

olive oil
150g (5 oz or 1 bunch) young swiss chard (silverbeet) or young ruby chard (red swiss chard), stems removed
100g (3½ oz or 1 bunch) baby english spinach, stems removed
salt/pepper

Heat a heavy-based pan over high heat, add a little olive oil, then the greens. Season with salt and black pepper and sauté quickly, stirring, until leaves just begin to wilt. Serve immediately.

To prepare this salad in advance combine all ingredients except the bread, basil and vinaigrette. When ready to serve, add bread and basil to salad and mix together with the vinaigrette.

Panzanella

Serves 6

2 red and 2 yellow peppers (capsicum), roasted, peeled and sliced (Basics page 164)
red wine vinaigrette (Basics page 171)
6 vine-ripened tomatoes, blanched and skinned
1 red onion, thinly sliced
1 red chilli, finely chopped
1 cup basil leaves
$^{1}/_{2}$ cup (75g or 2$^{1}/_{2}$ oz) ligurian or kalamata olives
8 anchovy fillets, drained and halved lengthwise
1 tablespoon salted capers, well rinsed
$^{1}/_{2}$ loaf ciabatta or other good italian bread, cut into large dice

Prepare roasted peppers and red wine vinaigrette as recipes direct.

Halve the tomatoes horizontally, then quarter each half.

In a large bowl, combine roasted peppers, tomatoes, onion, chilli, basil, olives, anchovies and capers and mix lightly. Add diced bread and enough of the vinaigrette to moisten.

Couscous

Serves 6

$^{1}/_{2}$ salted lemon, flesh discarded and skin finely diced (Basics page 173)
3 cups (560g/1 lb 4 oz) instant couscous
$^{1}/_{2}$ cup (75g /2$^{1}/_{2}$ oz) dried currants
$^{1}/_{2}$ cup (60g/2 oz) slivered almonds, roasted
1 tablespoon unsalted butter
1 teaspoon ground cinnamon (good quality)
pinch of saffron threads
salt/pepper
750ml (1$^{1}/_{4}$ pt) chicken stock, boiling (Basics page 176)
$^{1}/_{2}$ cup coriander leaves, chopped

Prepare salted lemon as recipe directs.

Combine couscous, salted lemon, currants, almonds, butter, cinnamon, saffron, salt and black pepper in a large bowl. Add the stock and stir until well mixed. Cover tightly with plastic food wrap and allow to steam for 10 minutes. Remove cover and stir well. Taste and adjust seasoning if required. Mix in coriander leaves just before serving.

Sometimes at the restaurant we serve wet polenta topped with shaved parmesan and a spoonful of pesto. Alternatively omit parmesan and fold through 80g (3 oz) gorgonzola.

Wet polenta

Serves 6

1 litre (1³/₄ pt) full-cream milk
¹/₂ onion
few sprigs thyme
1 sprig rosemary
2 bay leaves
4 cloves garlic, halved
110g (4 oz) polenta (yellow cornmeal)
60g (2 oz) parmesan, freshly grated
1 tablespoon unsalted butter
salt/pepper

Place milk, onion, herbs and garlic in a saucepan and bring to almost boiling. Place polenta in a large, heavy-based saucepan, strain infused milk onto polenta and whisk until blended.

Stir constantly over moderate heat until mixture returns to the boil. Reduce heat to very low and cook, stirring often, for 20-30 minutes or until polenta is cooked and thickened. Fold in parmesan and butter and season to taste with salt and black pepper.

Polenta is best served as soon as possible however, if you should need to cook and hold polenta, try this method: Prepare polenta as directed, except omit the parmesan, butter and seasonings. Allow polenta to cool, then cover and refrigerate until needed. To reheat, heat a little extra milk in a saucepan and gradually whisk in the cold wet polenta. Heat through, then stir in cheese, butter and seasonings.

Try spreading grilled polenta with tapenade (Basics page 166) and topping with roasted field (open-flat or swiss brown) mushrooms.

Grilled polenta

Serves 6

Prepare wet polenta as directed above, except increase polenta to 175g (about 6 oz) and omit the parmesan and butter. Press cooked polenta into a greased baking dish to 1cm (¹/₂ in) thickness. Allow to cool, then cut into triangles.

Brush triangles with melted butter or olive oil and grill or barbecue until well-coloured and warmed through. Serve with toppings as desired.

If you prefer to cook your own dried borlotti beans, see recipe for cooking chickpeas, Basics page 164.

Tuscan bean stew

Serves 6

olive oil
3 shallots (french shallots), sliced
3 cloves garlic, crushed
1 tablespoon italian style tomato paste (concentrated purée)
2 teaspoons oregano leaves
2 teaspoons thyme leaves
125ml (4½ fl oz) white wine
8 roma (italian plum) tomatoes, skinned, seeded and diced
400g (13 oz) can roma (italian plum) tomatoes, diced, with juice
200ml (7 fl oz) chicken stock (Basics page 176)
3 cups (750g/1 lb 10 oz) cooked borlotti beans
salt/pepper
pinch of sugar

Heat a heavy-based saucepan over high heat, add a little olive oil and sauté shallots and garlic until transparent. Add tomato paste and herbs and cook briefly, stirring.

Deglaze pan with the wine and simmer until reduced by half. Add fresh and canned tomatoes and continue to cook for 5 minutes. Add stock and cook until reduced by one-third. Add drained, cooked beans and continue to reduce to desired consistency. Season with salt and black pepper and, if too acidic, sweeten with the sugar.

Red cabbage with bacon and hazelnuts

Serves 4

olive oil
1 onion, sliced
2 cloves garlic, crushed
½ red cabbage, shredded
125ml (4½ fl oz) red wine vinegar (see Glossary)
½ cup (90g/3 oz) brown sugar
½ cup flat-leaf parsley, shredded
8 thin rashers bacon, grilled until crisp
⅓ cup (50g/2 oz) hazelnuts, roasted and skinned

Heat a heavy-based pan over moderate heat and add a little olive oil. Add onion and garlic and sweat until onion is transparent. Add cabbage to pan and sauté until softened.

Add vinegar and brown sugar, mix lightly, cover and cook for 10 minutes. Remove lid and cook a further 5 minutes.

Just before serving, fold in parsley, then top with crisp bacon and scatter with hazelnuts.

These potatoes are sometimes listed on our menu as farmhouse or rosemary potatoes. This basic recipe can be altered with a number of flavour variations. You can achieve different looks and textures depending on whether the potatoes are sliced, quartered or cut into wedges.

Oven-roasted potatoes

Serves 6-8

10 medium potatoes such as sebago, washed (not peeled)
2 tablespoons extra-virgin olive oil
2 tablespoons rosemary leaves
2 tablespoons thyme leaves
3 cloves garlic, finely chopped
salt/pepper
2 tablespoons unsalted butter

Preheat oven to 200°C (400°F/Gas 6). Quarter potatoes, place in a bowl and toss through olive oil, rosemary, thyme and garlic. Spread potatoes onto an oven tray lined with baking (silicone) paper and season with salt and black pepper. Dot with butter and roast until tender and golden, about 30 minutes.

Variations
For Balsamic Potatoes: Slice potatoes into 1cm (1/2 in) rounds. Omit rosemary. Brush with 2 tablespoons balsamic vinegar as potatoes are removed from oven.

For Parmesan Potatoes: Slice potatoes into 1cm (1/2 in) rounds. Omit rosemary and butter. Roast until tender, about 20 minutes. Remove from oven, sprinkle with 1 cup (100g/3 oz) freshly grated parmesan and place under a preheated grill until golden.

Roasted southern golds, chorizo, chilli and coriander

Serves 4

2 dried chorizo sausages, sliced diagonally
2 tablespoons clarified butter (Basics page 164)
18 southern gold (pink-eye) potatoes, steamed, then quartered or halved, depending on size
salt/pepper
red chillies, to taste, sliced into rings
1 cup coriander leaves

Preheat oven to 200°C (400°F/Gas 6). Heat a heavy-based ovenproof pan over moderate heat (or use a flameproof casserole), add chorizo and sauté until well-coloured.

Add clarified butter to pan with the potatoes and sauté until golden. Season with salt and black pepper, then place pan in oven to roast for 10 minutes. Remove from oven and fold through sliced chilli and coriander leaves. Serve immediately.

See photograph page 111

Caponata

Serves 6

3 tablespoons olive oil
1 large eggplant (aubergine), diced
1 large red onion, diced
2 cloves garlic, chopped
2 sticks celery, diced
1 red and 1 yellow pepper (capsicum), seeded and diced
60ml (2 fl oz) red wine vinegar (see Glossary)
400g (13 oz) can roma (italian plum) tomatoes, chopped, with juice
2 teaspoons sugar
1/3 cup (60g/2 oz) pitted and chopped green and/or black olives
1 tablespoon salted capers, well rinsed
salt/pepper
3 tablespoons flat-leaf parsley, shredded

Heat oil in a wide, heavy-based saucepan and sauté eggplant until golden. Remove eggplant from pan.

Add onion to pan and sauté until golden, add garlic and cook a further 2 minutes, adding a little more oil if required. Add celery and peppers and cook 5 minutes more. Deglaze pan with vinegar, then add tomatoes with their liquid and sugar, stir well.

Cook, uncovered, until mixture is fairly dry. Return eggplant to pan with the olives and capers, mix well and season to taste. Cook a further 5 minutes, then remove from heat. Stir through parsley. Serve either warm or cold.

Tabbouli

Serves 6

1/2 cup (90g/3 oz) burghul (see Glossary)
250ml (9 fl oz) cold water
1 cup flat-leaf parsley, chopped
1/4 cup mint leaves, chopped
2 cloves garlic, crushed
1 small red onion, finely diced
2 roma (italian plum) tomatoes, seeded and diced
60ml (2 fl oz) extra-virgin olive oil
60ml (2 fl oz) fresh lemon juice
salt/pepper

Soak burghul in cold water overnight.

Next day, stir in parsley, mint, garlic, onion, tomatoes, olive oil and lemon juice and mix lightly. Season with salt and black pepper.

Radicchio and bacon

Serves 6

3 small tight heads radicchio lettuce
olive oil
salt/pepper
knob of unsalted butter
balsamic vinegar
12 thin rashers bacon
3 tablespoons flat-leaf parsley, shredded

Cut each radicchio into 6 wedges. Heat a heavy-based pan over high heat, and add a little olive oil. Add radicchio to pan, season with salt and black pepper and sauté for 2 minutes. Add butter and a splash of balsamic to pan. Reduce heat, cover and cook until softened. Remove pan from heat.

Meanwhile, grill bacon until crisp and drain on absorbent paper. Add bacon and parsley to radicchio and serve immediately.

Sometimes we crumble goat's cheese or fetta over the beans.

Green beans with mustard cream

Serves 6

olive oil
2 shallots (french shallots), diced
1 clove garlic, crushed
125ml (4½ fl oz) chicken stock (Basics page 176)
250ml (9 fl oz) cream
1½ teaspoons dijon mustard
½ lemon, juice only
salt/pepper
350g (12 oz) french beans (stringless green)

Heat a heavy-based pan over high heat and add a little olive oil. Add shallots and garlic and sauté until transparent.

Add chicken stock, bring to the boil and boil until liquid reduces by half. Add cream, reduce heat to moderate and cook until liquid evaporates enough for sauce to coat the back of a spoon. Remove from heat and beat in mustard and lemon juice, then season with salt and black pepper.

Blanch beans in boiling salted water and drain well. Toss beans with hot mustard cream and spoon into a serving bowl.

See photograph page 111

Pumpkin, chilli, coriander and hommus

Serves 4

1.5kg (3½ lb) butternut pumpkin (butternut squash), peeled and seeded
extra-virgin olive oil
salt/pepper
2 teaspoons cumin seed, roasted and ground
¼ cup (45g/ 1½ oz) pepitas (see Glossary)
1 long red chilli (anaheim or jalapeno), thinly sliced diagonally
4 tablespoons hommus (Basics page 166)
½ cup coriander leaves

Preheat oven to 200°C (400°F/Gas 6). Cut pumpkin into large wedges and place on an oven tray lined with baking (silicone) paper. Drizzle pumpkin with a little oil and season with salt, pepper and ground cumin. Roast until tender, about 20 minutes, depending on wedge size.

Roast pepitas in a dry frying pan over moderate heat, tossing until slightly coloured.

To serve, place pumpkin in a serving bowl and scatter with the chilli. Top with pepitas, hommus and coriander leaves and season with a generous grinding of black pepper.

See photograph opposite page

Mushrooms, garlic, thyme and goat's cheese

Serves 4

extra-virgin olive oil
60g (2 oz) unsalted butter
3 cloves garlic
12 large swiss brown or flat mushrooms, wiped
salt/pepper
120g (4 oz) goat's cheese
several sprigs thyme, leaves removed
60g (2 oz) rocket, stems removed
1 tablespoon best quality balsamic vinegar

Preheat grill to high. Heat a heavy-based ovenproof pan over high heat, add a little olive oil and the butter. Add garlic, toss, then add mushrooms, gills down. When half-cooked, turn mushrooms over and season liberally with salt and black pepper.

Crumble a little goat's cheese in the centre of each mushroom and sprinkle with fresh thyme. Place mushrooms under preheated grill and cook until cheese is warm.

To serve, arrange a bed of rocket on each plate, top each with three mushrooms and drizzle with balsamic vinegar.

Pumpkin, chilli, coriander and hommus (recipe page 128)

Left: Banana tarte tatin with rum and raisin ice cream (recipe page 135)

Above: Mascarpone and white chocolate torte with mixed berries (recipe page 144)

desserts

Left: Grilled peach, toasted brioche, amaretto and yoghurt *(recipe page 155)*

A variation is to serve this cheesecake with grilled bananas and a drizzle of caramel sauce. To prepare bananas, halve lengthwise, brush with a little butter, sprinkle with brown sugar and place under a preheated grill until caramelised.

Baked cheesecake with balsamic strawberries

Serves 8

You will need a 1 x 24cm (9½ in) cake ring for this recipe (Notes page 179)

sweet shortcrust pastry (Basics page 175)

675g (1 lb 8 oz) cream cheese (preferably Kraft, not light)
2 eggs
2 lemons, grated zest only
3 tablespoons cornflour
1 teaspoon vanilla essence
225g (8 oz) caster sugar
300ml (11 fl oz) cream

balsamic strawberries

3 heaped tablespoons icing sugar
90ml (3 fl oz) cointreau
good dash (1-2 teaspoons) best quality balsamic vinegar
250g (9 oz) strawberries, washed, hulled and halved

Prepare pastry as recipe directs.

Preheat oven to 190°C (375°F/Gas 5). Roll out pastry to a circle at least 28cm (11 in) diameter, 4mm (⅛ in) thick, and place flat on an oven tray lined with baking (silicone) paper. Bake 10-12 minutes until golden. Remove tray from oven and press cake ring into pastry to cut to shape. Discard excess pastry.

Reduce oven temperature to 120°C (250°F/Gas 1/2). In a food processor, beat cream cheese until smooth, then add eggs, lemon zest, cornflour, vanilla and sugar, mix well. Remove mixture to a bowl and using a firm whisk, fold in cream. Pour filling into cake ring and bake for 15-20 minutes – the filling will change colour slightly but will not be completely set. Remove from oven and cool.

For the strawberries, at least one hour before serving, combine icing sugar, cointreau and vinegar, then pour over berries. Accompany a slice of cheesecake with a spoonful of macerated berries.

caramel sauce

250g (9 oz) caster sugar
60ml (2 fl oz) water
250ml (9 fl oz) cream
½ lemon, strained juice only

Combine sugar and water in a small saucepan and stir over moderate heat until sugar dissolves. Bring to the boil, stirring occasionally, then do not stir again, but boil until syrup becomes a dark golden colour. Immediately remove from heat and very carefully, as hot syrup will spit, stir in cream and lemon juice. Return pan to heat and stir until caramel is smooth.

In this recipe we like to use Bundaburg Rum. It is a dark, full-flavoured rum well known by Queenslanders. I suggest that unless you have a lot of time on your hands you buy a high quality butter puff pastry from a good patisserie or the supermarket.

Banana tarte tatin with rum and raisin ice cream

Serves 6

250g (9 oz) caster sugar
60ml (2 fl oz) water
80ml (3 fl oz) dark rum
60ml (2 fl oz) cream
6 large bananas, sliced thickly, diagonally
6 x 10cm (4 in) circles butter puff pastry
1 egg, beaten, for egg wash
rum and raisin ice cream (page 160)

Butter 6 x 10cm (4 in) tart tins and place on an oven tray lined with baking (silicone) paper. Preheat oven to 220°C (425°F/Gas 7).

Combine sugar and water in a small saucepan and stir over low heat until sugar dissolves. Bring to the boil and boil without stirring until syrup turns a dark caramel colour. Immediately remove from heat and very carefully, as caramel spits, stir in the rum. Return to low heat and stir until smooth, then add the cream and bring to the boil.

Pour an equal quantity of caramel into the base of each tart tin. Arrange sliced banana in concentric circles on top of caramel, then top each with a puff pastry circle. Egg wash pastry by brushing with beaten egg. Take care not to let egg wash run down edge of pastry. Bake for 10-12 minutes or until pastry is golden.

To serve, remove tarts from oven and while still quite hot, invert tarts onto centre of serving plates. Top each tart with a spoonful of rum and raisin ice cream.

See photograph page 130

Bitter chocolate torte and espresso ice cream

Serves 12

250g (9 oz) dark (66% cocoa butter) couverture, roughly chopped (see Glossary)
250g (9 oz) whole blanched almonds
250g (9 oz) unsalted butter, softened
250g (9 oz) caster sugar
8 eggs, separated
icing sugar
espresso ice cream (page 160)

Preheat oven to 150°C (300°F/Gas 2). Place coverture in a bowl over gently simmering water and allow to melt, stirring occasionally, until smooth. Cool slightly. Place almonds in a food processor and pulse briefly until coarsely chopped.

In a mixing bowl, cream butter and sugar until light and fluffy. Beat in egg yolks, one at a time, until blended. Fold through almonds and melted chocolate. Whisk egg whites to soft peaks then fold into chocolate mixture.

Pour mixture into a greased and baking (silicone) paper-lined cake tin, 32cm (12¾ in) diameter, 4cm (1¾ in) deep (or use a 32cm quiche tin with fluted sides). Bake for 45 minutes or until firm to the touch – if you are unsure, turn heat off and allow torte to cool in the oven with the door slightly ajar. The top will have a cracked appearance. Store in an airtight container at room temperature.

To serve, dust torte with icing sugar. Slice into wedges and accompany with espresso ice cream or a spoonful of double cream.

See photograph page 151

Pears are best cooked one day in advance to allow flavours to infuse.

Cassis poached pears with spice cake

Serves 6

6 firm pears, peeled, leaving stems attached
1 lemon, zest removed in strips
1 cinnamon quill
200g (7 oz) caster sugar
600ml (21 fl oz) water
200ml (7 fl oz) crème de cassis
600ml (21 fl oz) red wine
mascarpone

spice cake

100g ($3^1/_2$ oz) unsalted butter, softened
250g (9 oz) soft brown sugar
3 eggs, beaten lightly
220g ($7^3/_4$ oz) plain flour
2 tablespoons ground almonds
1 tablespoon baking powder
1 teaspoon ground cinnamon
1 teaspoon cardamom seeds, roasted and ground
$^1/_2$ teaspoon ground cloves
$^1/_2$ orange, grated zest only
2 teaspoons crystallised ginger, finely chopped
200ml (7 fl oz) milk
1 orange, juice only
2 tablespoons fine-cut orange marmalade
icing sugar

Select a saucepan that will fit the pears snugly. Combine lemon zest, cinnamon, sugar, water, crème de cassis and wine in the pan. Place over moderate heat and stir until sugar dissolves, then bring to a simmer. Halve pears and scoop out the cores using a melon baller or teaspoon. Add pears to syrup, place an inverted plate over pears to keep them submerged. Poach until tender. Remove from heat and allow pears to cool slightly in syrup.

Remove pears from syrup and place in a bowl. Bring syrup to the boil and boil until reduced by two-thirds. Pour syrup over pears and refrigerate until ready to serve.

Preheat oven to 160°C (325°/Gas 3). Line a 20cm (8 in) round springform tin with baking (silicone) paper .

In a mixing bowl, cream butter and brown sugar together until light and fluffy. Beat in eggs, one at a time, until blended. Combine the flour, almonds, baking powder, spices, orange zest and ginger well and fold into batter. Mix in milk, orange juice and marmalade, then pour batter into prepared tin and bake for 50-60 minutes until cake pulls away from sides of tin. When cool, store cake in an airtight container at room temperature.

To serve, dust spice cake liberally with sifted icing sugar, then cut two narrow wedges of cake per serve. Arrange slices by overlapping them on a plate, place two pear halves alongside and top with a little reduced poaching syrup. Accompany with a spoonful of mascarpone.

Although most restaurants feature a lemon or citrus tart, good ones are thin on the ground. The most important aspect of a good lemon tart is to ensure that the custard is just set, giving a smooth velvety texture. Overcooking results in air bubbles throughout, giving it a grainy texture. Equally refreshing is the passionfruit variation listed below.

Citrus tart with mascarpone

Serves 8

1 x 24cm (9½ in) blind-baked sweet shortcrust pastry shell (Basics page 175)

300ml (11 fl oz) cream

9 eggs

375g (13 oz) caster sugar

5 lemons, grated zest of 3, juice of 5

caster sugar, for caramelising or icing sugar, for dusting

mascarpone, beaten lightly

Prepare pastry shell as recipe directs.

Preheat oven to 110°C (225°F/Gas 1/4). Place cream in a small saucepan and bring almost to the boil. In a bowl, lightly whisk eggs and sugar together, whisk in the hot cream then the lemon juice. Strain mixture into a pouring jug and allow to rest for 10 minutes before skimming off any foam from the surface. Stir in lemon zest.

Pour filling into prebaked tart shell and bake for 50-60 minutes or until filling is barely set – it will continue to set whilst cooling. Remove from oven and allow to cool at room temperature.

To serve, cut tart into portions and sprinkle liberally with caster sugar. Caramelise tops by using a kitchen blowtorch (alternatively, omit caster sugar and dust with sifted icing sugar). Place tart wedge on a serving plate and add a spoonful of mascarpone to one side.

See photograph page 152

For passionfruit tart

300ml (11 fl oz) cream

300g (11 oz) caster sugar

8 eggs

300ml (11 fl oz) passionfruit pulp, pulsed lightly in a food processor and strained

Use the same method as above, adding the strained passionfruit instead of the lemon juice.

Biscotti can be cooked well ahead of time and stored in an airtight jar. Creamed rice is best served at room temperature on the day it is made. It could be served warm but it is far too rich straight from the refrigerator.

Creamed rice, mango, basil and biscotti

Serves 6

60g (2 oz) unsalted butter
90g (3 oz) caster sugar
125g (4½ oz) short grain rice
1 vanilla pod, split lengthwise and scraped
500ml (18 fl oz) milk
500ml (18 fl oz) cream
pinch of salt
3 mangoes
basil leaves, shredded

biscotti

250g (9 oz) plain flour
¼ teaspoon baking powder
pinch of salt
250g (9 oz) caster sugar
2 eggs, beaten lightly
½ teaspoon grated orange zest
¼ teaspoon vanilla essence
100g (3½ oz) shelled, unsalted pistachios
75g (2½ oz) pine nuts

For the biscotti, preheat oven to 160°C (325°F/Gas 3). Sieve flour, baking powder and salt together into a bowl and stir in sugar. Make a well in the centre and add eggs, orange zest and vanilla. Gently mix to combine, then stir in pistachios and pine nuts.

On a floured surface, form mixture into a rectangular shape and place on an oven tray lined with baking (silicone) paper. Make sure shape is well formed to ensure it holds together. Bake for 45 minutes or until golden. Remove from oven and cool completely.

Cut biscotti shape into very thin slices, about 2-3mm (⅛ in) thick, and lay slices flat on oven trays. Return to very cool electric oven, approximately 80°C (175°F) to dry biscotti until crisp. Alternatively biscotti may be dried overnight in a gas oven with just the pilot light on.

For the rice, preheat oven to 160°C (325°F/Gas 3). Melt butter in a heavy-based saucepan over low heat, then add sugar and rice, stir for 5 minutes. Stir in vanilla scrapings, milk, cream and salt and bring to the boil.

Pour mixture into an ovenproof dish approximately 23 x 26 cm (8 x 10½ in) and cover with foil. Place dish into a water bath and bake for 2 hours, stirring every 30 minutes until rice is soft and creamy. Remove dish from oven and stir occasionally while cooling.

To serve, slice mango cheeks from either side of the stone and, using a large metal spoon, ease it between the skin and flesh to remove cheek in one piece. Place a mango cheek on each serving plate with a large spoonful of cooled creamed rice on the side. Scatter shredded basil over mango and accompany with two biscotti.

This cake has gone through many changes in the past several years. It originally contained flour, but when Air New Zealand requested a flourless cake, we increased the orange pulp and almonds and removed the flour and ended up with this recipe which is moist and delicious.

Crushed orange and almond cake

Serves 8

orange confit (Basics page 173)
2 oranges, seedless
250g (9 oz) unsalted butter, softened
250g (9 oz) caster sugar
6 eggs, separated
1 tablespoon baking powder, sifted
300g (10 oz) ground almonds
icing sugar
crème fraîche

Prepare orange confit as recipe directs.

Place oranges in a saucepan and cover with water. Invert a plate over oranges to keep them submerged. Bring to the boil and simmer until oranges are very soft. Drain, then quarter (and make sure there are no seeds). Pulse oranges briefly in a food processor until coarsely chopped, measure out 300ml (11 fl oz) of the orange pulp.

Preheat oven to 200°C (450°F/Gas 6). Grease and line a 24cm (9½ in) round springform tin with baking (silicone) paper.

In a mixing bowl, cream butter and sugar together well. Add egg yolks, one at a time, beating well between each addition. Combine baking powder and almonds and add alternately with the orange pulp to creamed mixture. Finally, whisk egg whites to soft peaks and carefully fold into batter.

Pour mixture into prepared tin and bake for 10 minutes. Reduce oven temperature to 160°C (325°F/Gas 3) and continue to bake for 50-60 minutes longer until cake pulls away from sides of tin. This cake is best served at room temperature and should be stored in an airtight container.

To serve, dust cake with sifted icing sugar. Place a slice of cake just off centre on serving plates. Arrange a stack of 4-5 slices of orange confit alongside, drizzle with a little of the orange confit syrup and accompany with a spoonful of crème fraîche.

Try serving this tart with grilled ripe peaches or fresh raspberries. The staff at e'cco are addicted to this tart with a cup of coffee.

Baked custard tart with toffied mango

Serves 10

one 24cm (9½ in) blind-baked sweet shortcrust tart shell (Basics page 175)

1 vanilla pod, split

1 cinnamon quill

500ml (18 fl oz) full cream milk

500ml (18 fl oz) cream

300g (10 oz) caster sugar

7 eggs

caramel syrup

250g (9 oz) caster sugar

60ml (2 fl oz) water

125ml (4½ fl oz) orange juice, freshly squeezed

toffied mangoes

5 mangoes

caster sugar, extra

Prepare pastry shell as recipe directs.

Preheat oven to 120°C (250°F/Gas 1/2). Combine vanilla pod, cinnamon quill, milk, cream and 150 g (5 oz) of the sugar in a saucepan and bring almost to the boil, stirring to dissolve the sugar. In a bowl, lightly whisk remaining sugar and eggs together. Whisk hot milk mixture into eggs and strain into a pouring jug. Allow mixture to stand for 10 minutes and skim off any foam that rises to the surface.

Pour custard into prebaked tart shell and bake for 40-50 minutes, or until filling is just set. Allow to cool in tin and serve at room temperature.

For caramel syrup, combine sugar and water in a small saucepan over moderate heat and stir until sugar dissolves. Bring to the boil and boil until syrup becomes a deep golden colour. Do not allow it to burn. Immediately remove from heat and very carefully, as mixture will spit, add orange juice. Return pan to low heat and stir until syrup is smooth.

For mangoes, slice cheeks from each side of mango stones and, using a very large metal spoon, insert it between flesh and skin of cheek and ease flesh out. Lay cheeks on an oven tray and sprinkle liberally with extra caster sugar. Using a kitchen blow torch, or under a very hot grill, caramelise the sugar.

To serve, place a wedge of tart on each serving plate. Lay a caramelised mango cheek to one side. Drizzle thin caramel syrup over and around mango cheek.

Any selection of available citrus fruit works well in this compote.

Lime and mascarpone tart with citrus compote

Serves 6

six 10 x 2cm (4 x 3/4 in) blind-baked sweet shortcrust tart shells (Basics page 175)
8 egg yolks
100ml (3 1/2 fl oz) lime juice
250g (9 oz) caster sugar
250g (9 oz) unsalted butter
150g (5 oz) mascarpone
extra mascarpone, beaten lightly

citrus compote

1 blood orange, if available
2 oranges, seedless
2 limes
1 grapefruit
1 lemon
250g (9 oz) caster sugar
250ml (9 fl oz) water
1/2 cinnamon quill
1/2 vanilla pod, split and scraped
3 slices fresh ginger
1 kaffir lime leaf (see Glossary)
1 earl grey tea bag

For the compote, wash fruit well, remove zest from half the fruit with a zester or stiff-bladed peeler, then cut into fine strips. Peel fruit, including pith, then slice fruit into 1cm (1/2 in)-thick rounds.

Combine sugar, water, zest, cinnamon, vanilla pod and scrapings, ginger, lime leaf and tea bag in a large saucepan. Place over moderate heat and stir until sugar dissolves, then slowly bring to the boil. Reduce heat and simmer for 10 minutes, then pour syrup over sliced fruit. Cover and cool to room temperature. Refrigerate until needed.

Prepare tart shells as recipe directs.

For the filling, combine egg yolks, lime juice and sugar in the top of a double saucepan (double boiler) or in a heatproof bowl placed over gently simmering water and stir. Add butter and whisk until thick and glossy – this will take about 20 minutes before mixture no longer tastes of egg. Remove from heat and cool lime butter, then fold through the 150g (5 oz) mascarpone. Pour mixture into tart shells.

To serve, spoon an assortment of fruit and syrup onto centre of plates. Place tart on fruit and top with a small spoonful of mascarpone.

See photograph page 150

Serve both these recipes at room temperature. Once refrigerated the texture will be quite solid because of the high chocolate and butter content.

Chocolate and macadamia brownie with white chocolate ice cream

Serves 12

280g (10 oz) unsalted butter, softened
500g (17 oz) caster sugar
5 eggs
30ml (1 fl oz) light corn syrup
185g (6½ oz) plain flour
125g (4½ oz) cocoa powder
185 g (6½ oz) raisins
185g (6½ oz) dark couverture buttons, chopped (see Glossary)
85-90g (3 oz) unsalted macadamias, chopped
icing sugar
white chocolate ice cream (page 160)

Preheat oven to 150°C (300°F/Gas 2). Line a 23 x 30 x 4cm (9 x 12 x 2¾ in) baking tin with baking (silicone) paper.

In a bowl, cream butter and sugar together until light and fluffy. Beat in eggs, one at a time, then mix in corn syrup. Sift together flour and cocoa and fold into mixture. Mix through raisins, chocolate and macadamias. Pour batter into prepared tin and bake for 50-60 minutes. Cool.

To serve, cut brownies into large squares and dust with sifted icing sugar. Plate and accompany with a large spoonful of white chocolate ice cream.

Chocolate tart with burnt caramel ice cream

Serves 8

one 24cm (9½ in) blind-baked sweet shortcrust tart shell (Basics page 175)
375g (13 oz) dark (66% cocoa mass) couverture, chopped roughly (see Glossary)
250g (9 oz) unsalted butter
3 eggs
5 egg yolks
75g (2½ oz) caster sugar
burnt caramel ice cream (page 161)

Prepare pastry shell as recipe directs.

Place coverture and butter in a bowl over gently simmering water and allow to melt, stirring occasionally, until smooth. Cool.

Preheat oven to 150°C (300°F/Gas 2). In an electric mixer bowl, whisk eggs and egg yolks with caster sugar until thick and pale and carefully fold into cooled chocolate mixture. Pour custard into tart shell and bake for 12 minutes. Remove from oven and allow to rest for 1 hour.

To serve, slice tart into wedges and accompany with burnt caramel ice cream.

I'm not usually one for altering classics, however we adapted this recipe from tiramisu and it went on to become one of our most popular desserts.

Mascarpone and white chocolate torte with mixed berries

Serves 10

1½ leaves gelatine (see Glossary)
125ml (4½ fl oz) cold water
2 tablespoons cream
5 eggs, separated
100g (3½ oz) caster sugar
1 lemon, grated zest only
500g (17 oz) mascarpone
400g (13 oz) savoiardi (sponge fingers; preferably italian)
250g (9 oz) assorted fresh berries (raspberries, blueberries, halved strawberries)
220g (8 oz) best quality white chocolate, grated
300ml (11 fl oz) cream, whipped lightly
500g (17 oz) additional mixed fresh berries

raspberry coulis

500g (17 oz) fresh or frozen raspberries
200g (7 oz) caster sugar
250ml (9 fl oz) water
1-2 tablespoons cointreau

To make the coulis, combine raspberries, sugar and water in a small saucepan and bring to the boil. Remove pan from heat and purée mixture in a blender. Pass through a fine sieve to remove all seeds, then stir in cointreau and set aside.

Line the base and sides of a 24cm (9½ in) springform tin with baking (silicone) paper. Soak gelatine leaves in the cold water until they soften. Heat 2 tablespoons cream in a small saucepan until almost boiling. Remove gelatine leaves from water, squeeze tightly, add to hot cream and stir until dissolved.

In a mixing bowl, beat egg yolks, sugar and lemon zest together until thick and pale. Stir in mascarpone until just combined, then fold in gelatine mixture. Discard one egg white, then whisk remaining whites to soft peaks and carefully fold through mascarpone mixture.

Lightly soak savoiardi in half the warm raspberry coulis before placing in a single layer in base of prepared tin. Spread with half the mascarpone mixture, sprinkle with 1 cup of the berries and half the white chocolate. Repeat with remaining ingredients to make a second layer. Cover and refrigerate torte for several hours or overnight before serving.

To serve, cut torte into wedges and place on serving plates. Top with a spoonful of whipped cream. Moisten additional berries with remaining raspberry coulis and spoon alongside.

See photograph page 131

The quantity of gelatine used is crucial to a good panna cotta. This recipe has only enough gelatine for the panna cotta to just hold shape, bulging slightly. They must be turned out just before serving as they will only hold shape for a short time. At e'cco we use the small Nestlé plastic dariole moulds because they are pliable and make turning out the panna cotta much easier. The panna cotta can be scented by greasing the mould with almond oil or, alternatively, infusing the cream with a handful of blanched almonds while bringing it to the boil.

Panna cotta with charred mango cheeks

Serves 6

2 leaves gelatine
80ml (3 fl oz) cold milk
450ml (16 fl oz) cream
60g (2 oz) caster sugar
1/2 vanilla pod, split lengthwise
1/2 lemon, grated zest only
60ml (2 fl oz) white rum
2 tablespoons unsalted butter, melted
3 mangoes
caramel syrup from baked custard tart with toffied mango (page 141)

Soak gelatine in cold milk in a bowl to soften. Combine 1 cup (250ml/9 fl oz) of the cream, the sugar, vanilla pod and lemon zest in a saucepan and bring almost to the boil. Remove pan from heat. Strain onto softened gelatine and milk mixture and stir to dissolve completely. Add rum to mixture and allow to stand until room temperature.

Whip remaining 200ml (7 fl oz) cream to soft peaks and gently fold into cooled mixture. Pour into six greased 1/2 cup (125ml/4 1/2 fl oz) dariole moulds and refrigerate overnight.

To serve, prepare caramel syrup as recipe directs. Preheat grill to high. Slice cheeks from each side of mango stones and, using a very large metal spoon, insert it between flesh and skin of cheek and ease flesh out. Brush lightly with melted butter and char-grill mango cheeks using a ridged pan (or use a barbecue) over high heat.

To serve, run a knife around the edge of dariole moulds, then gently shake panna cotta out onto serving plates. Accompany each with a mango cheek. Drizzle caramel sauce over and around the mango.

A variation for fresh pears or apricots appears below when fresh sweet cherries are out of season.

Cherry and almond cobbler with coconut ice cream

Serves 6

1kg (2 lb 3 oz) fresh sweet cherries, pitted
100g ($3^1/_2$ oz) caster sugar
50ml (2 fl oz) water
30ml (1 fl oz) kirsch
icing sugar, for dusting
coconut ice cream (page 160)

cobbler topping

310g (11 oz) plain flour
pinch of salt
1 tablespoon baking powder
100g ($3^1/_2$ oz) caster sugar
75g ($2^1/_2$ oz) unsalted butter, diced
100g ($3^1/_2$ oz) flaked almonds
400ml (14 fl oz) cream
additional caster sugar

Combine 400g (13 oz) of the cherries in a food processor with the sugar, water and kirsch, process to a purée. Divide remaining cherries between six x 10cm (4 in) tart tins and top with cherry purée.

For topping, preheat oven to 180°C (350°F/Gas 4). Combine flour, salt, baking powder and sugar in a bowl and rub in the butter until mixture resembles breadcrumbs. Add flaked almonds, then stir in cream to form a soft dough. Spoon topping over fruit in dishes and dust with additional caster sugar. Bake for 8 minutes, then reduce oven temperature to 150°C (300°F/Gas 2) and continue to bake for 10-15 minutes, or until golden.

To serve, remove cobblers from tins and place on dinner plates, dust with icing sugar and accompany with coconut ice cream.

For fresh pear or apricot cobbler

6 ripe pears or 12 large apricots
1 lemon, juice only
125g ($4^1/_2$ oz) caster sugar

Quarter and core pears or apricots then thinly slice. Toss in lemon juice and sugar and place fruit in base of tart tins. Top with cobbler topping and bake as directed above. This version is delicious served with burnt caramel ice cream (page 161).

Poached peaches are best used within a day.

Poached peaches, pistachio ice cream and honey champagne cream

Serves 6

900g (2 lb) caster sugar
1 vanilla pod, split lengthwise
1 litre (1³/₄ pt) water
6 peaches, firm but not green
pistachio ice cream (page 160)

honey champagne cream

250ml (9 fl oz) cream
1 tablespoon honey
1 teaspoon lemon juice
champagne

tuilles

50g (1³/₄ oz) unsalted butter, softened
110g (4 oz) caster sugar
110g (4 oz) plain flour
4 egg whites
50g (1³/₄ oz) shelled unsalted pistachios, finely chopped

To make tuilles, preheat oven to 160°C (325°F/Gas 3). In a mixing bowl, cream butter and sugar until light and fluffy. Add flour and egg whites, beating until smooth. Draw three 10cm (4 in) circles on baking (silicone) paper and invert paper over an oven tray.

Using a spatula, smear a thin layer of batter onto each circle, then sprinkle lightly with pistachios. Bake for 3-5 minutes until well-browned at the edges and golden in the centre. Remove from oven and, working quickly using a clean palate knife or spatula, carefully remove one tuille and mould by placing over a rolling pin to curl. Repeat with second and third tuille – if they become too hard to remove, return tray briefly to the oven to soften. Repeat process with remaining batter for remaining tuilles. Cool, then store in an airtight container until ready to use.

To poach peaches, place sugar, vanilla pod and water in a large saucepan and stir over low heat until sugar dissolves. Bring to the boil and boil for 5 minutes.

Place peaches in hot syrup and cover with a double thickness of greaseproof or baking (silicone) paper placed directly on top of syrup to keep peaches submerged. Poach until just soft, remembering they will continue to cook until cool. Remove with a slotted spoon and, when cool enough to handle, peel off skins and place in a bowl. Boil poaching syrup until it reduces by half, cool, then pour over peaches.

For honey champagne cream, whip cream, honey and lemon juice until soft peaks form. Add a little champagne and balance flavour with some of the poaching syrup. Mixture will thicken on standing in refrigerator and can be thinned with either more champagne or poaching syrup.

To serve, place one peach in each wide, flat serving bowl. Sit a large spoonful each of pistachio ice cream and honey champagne cream alongside and serve with tuilles.

Tiramisu

Serves 8-10

5 egg yolks
100g (3½ oz) caster sugar
500g (17 oz) mascarpone
4 egg whites
400ml (14 fl oz) hot espresso coffee (or use strong plunger coffee)
30ml (1 fl oz) galliano
30ml (1 fl oz) tia maria
30ml (1 fl oz) brandy
400g (13 oz) savoiardi (sponge fingers; preferably italian)
200g (7 oz) best quality dark chocolate, shaved
250ml (9 fl oz) cream, softly whipped
cocoa powder

In a mixing bowl, beat egg yolks and sugar until thick and pale then stir in mascarpone until well combined. Whisk egg whites to soft peaks and fold into mascarpone mixture.

Place a 24 x 4 cm (9½ x 1¾ in) cake ring (see Glossary) on a baking (silicone) paper-lined flat tray (or use a springform tin of similar size). Combine coffee, galliano, tia maria and brandy in a bowl. Dip half the savoiardi into this mixture, ensuring they do not become totally saturated, and arrange in a radial pattern inside the ring (or in the bottom of the tin). Cover with half the mascarpone mixture and sprinkle liberally with half the shaved chocolate. Repeat layers with remaining savoiardi, mascarpone and chocolate. Cover and refrigerate overnight.

To serve, place a wedge or large spoonful of tiramisu in the centre of each plate, top with whipped cream and dust generously with cocoa.

Pineapple coconut cake with pineapple sorbet

Serves 10

3 eggs
325g (11½ oz) caster sugar
pinch of salt
2 tablespoons extra-virgin olive oil
2 oranges, grated zest only
285g (10 oz) plain flour
2 teaspoons baking powder
350g (12 oz) pineapple flesh, thinly sliced, then diced
90g (3 oz) desiccated coconut, tightly packed
pineapple sorbet (page 162)

Preheat oven to 190°C (375°F/Gas 5). Line the base and sides of a 26cm (10½ in) springform tin with baking (silicone) paper.

In a mixing bowl, cream eggs and caster sugar together until light and fluffy. Beat in salt, olive oil and orange zest. Sift together flour and baking powder and fold into mixture, then fold through pineapple and coconut.

Pour batter into prepared tin and bake for 50-60 minutes or until golden.

To serve, accompany wedges of warm cake with pineapple sorbet.

Right: Tiramisu (recipe this page)

Above: Lime and mascarpone tart with citrus compote (recipe page 142)

Right: Bitter chocolate torte (recipe page 136)

Citrus tart with mascarpone
(recipe page 138)

The fig compote can be made well ahead. Store in an airtight container in the refrigerator until ready to use.

Sauternes custard with spiced fig compote

Serves 6

250g (9 oz) caster sugar
60ml (2 fl oz) cold water
2 tablespoons boiling water
1/2 vanilla pod, split lengthwise
350ml (12 fl oz) cream
2 eggs
5 egg yolks
100g (3 1/2 oz) additional caster sugar
120ml (4 fl oz) sauternes (dessert wine)

fig compote

400g (14 oz) dried figs
2 star anise
2 cinnamon quills
2 bay leaves
1 orange, zested into wide strips
1/2 teaspoon freshly ground black pepper
60g (2 oz) honey
125ml (4 1/2 fl oz) orange juice, freshly squeezed
250ml (9 fl oz) weak tea

For the compote, combine figs, star anise, cinnamon, bay leaves, orange zest, black pepper, honey, orange juice and tea in a saucepan over moderate heat and bring to the boil. Reduce heat and simmer 10 minutes. Remove from heat, cover and allow to cool to room temperature.

Combine sugar and cold water in a small saucepan over low heat and stir until sugar dissolves. Bring to the boil and boil without stirring until sugar caramelises. Swirl syrup around gently in saucepan if it is colouring unevenly. Watch carefully until syrup turns a dark gold, then immediately remove from heat and place pan in a bowl of iced water. Add the boiling water, mix until smooth then ladle caramel into base of six x 1/2 cup (125ml/4 fl oz) metal dariole moulds, dividing equally.

Preheat oven to 120°C (250°F/Gas 1/2). Scrape seeds from vanilla pod into a saucepan, add cream and vanilla pod and heat almost to the boil. In a bowl, lightly whisk eggs, yolks and additional sugar to combine. Add sauternes to hot cream, then whisk mixture into eggs. Strain through a fine sieve and allow custard to rest a few minutes, skimming off any foam as it rises.

Fill prepared moulds with custard and place in a baking dish. Half-fill dish with boiling water and bake until custards are just set, about 40 minutes. Remove from oven and allow custards to cool in water bath. Remove from water and refrigerate until cold.

To serve, run a knife around inside of mould to loosen custard. Invert onto serving plates and smooth the edges with a knife, if necessary. Arrange figs to one side with a little syrup.

The raspberry compote should be prepared just prior to serving so that the berries do not become too soft. This dessert is delicious served with either a spoonful of mascarpone, or vanilla bean ice cream (page 160).

Zabaglione torte with warm raspberry compote

Serves 10

12 eggs, separated
250g (9 oz) caster sugar
250g (9 oz) plain flour, sifted

filling

6 egg yolks
250g (9 oz) caster sugar
60g (2 oz) plain flour, sifted
250ml (9 fl oz) white wine
250ml (9 fl oz) dry sherry
3 cups (750ml/1¼ pt) cream, whipped
400ml (14 fl oz) hot espresso coffee (or use strong plunger coffee)
90ml (3 fl oz) galliano
icing sugar

raspberry compote

150ml (5 fl oz) sugar syrup (made with 125g/4 oz caster sugar dissolved in 180ml/6 fl oz water and boiled for 5 minutes)
150ml (5 fl oz) raspberry coulis (from mascarpone and white chocolate torte, page 144)
150ml (5 fl oz) crème de cassis
250g (9 oz) fresh raspberries

Preheat oven to 180°C (350°F/Gas 4). Line a 26cm (10½ in) springform tin with baking (silicone) paper. In a mixing bowl, whisk (or use an electric mixer) 12 egg yolks with 200g (7 oz) of the sugar until a pale yellow colour. Fold in flour. Combine egg whites with remaining 50g sugar and whisk to soft peaks then fold into the mixture. Pour batter into prepared tin and bake for 20 minutes or until golden. Remove from oven and allow cake to cool in tin.

For the filling, whisk together egg yolks and sugar until pale and stiff. Fold in the flour, then stir in wine and sherry. Place mixture in a double boiler (double saucepan) or in a heatproof bowl over gently simmering water and cook, whisking constantly, until mixture has thickened – do not allow mixture to boil. This will take 15-20 minutes. Remove from heat, allow to cool, then fold in whipped cream.

Remove sponge from springform, clean the tin and line it with plastic food wrap, allowing wrap to overhang edges generously. Invert cake and slice horizontally into four equal layers. Place bottom layer back into lined tin.

Combine hot coffee and galliano and brush liberally over this cake layer. Top this bottom layer with one-third of the filling. Repeat, layering with remaining sponge and filling, finishing with the fourth layer of sponge. Seal cake with overhanging wrap, place a weight on top and refrigerate for several hours or overnight.

For the compote, combine sugar syrup, raspberry coulis and cassis in a small saucepan and bring to the boil. Add raspberries and remove from heat.

To serve, place a wedge of cake on a plate and top with a little raspberry compote. Dust with icing sugar and serve immediately with mascarpone or vanilla bean ice cream.

Grilled peach, toasted brioche, amaretto and yoghurt

Serves 6

6 ripe peaches
caster sugar
1 x 500g (17 oz) brioche, thickly sliced (see Glossary)
icing sugar
185g (6½ oz) greek-style or sheep's milk natural yoghurt

amaretto sauce

250g (9 oz) caster sugar
125ml (4½ fl oz) water
125ml (4½ fl oz) amaretto

For the amaretto sauce, combine sugar and water in a small saucepan over moderate heat and stir until sugar dissolves. Bring to the boil and boil until syrup turns a golden colour. Immediately remove from heat and carefully, as mixture will spit, add amaretto. Return saucepan to heat and stir until syrup is smooth and returns to boil. Strain syrup and cool.

Preheat grill to very high. Halve peaches and discard stones. Sprinkle cut surface of peaches liberally with sugar and place on a greased oven tray. Place under grill until peaches caramelise.

Toast brioche lightly, cut slices diagonally in half and dust with icing sugar.

To serve, place two peach halves on each plate, rest brioche next to peaches. Place a spoonful of yoghurt between peaches and brioche and drizzle amaretto sauce over and around peaches.

See photograph page 132

Panettone pudding with blueberries and crème fraîche

Serves 8

1 x 500g (17 oz) panettone (see Glossary)
250g (9 oz) fresh blueberries
1 vanilla pod, split lengthwise
1 litre (1 3/4 pt) cream
6 eggs
250g (9 oz) caster sugar
crème fraîche (see Glossary)

Preheat oven to 120°C (250°F/Gas 1/2). Halve panettone from top to bottom, place flat on a board and slice crosswise about 1cm (1/2 in) thick. Discard ends. Lightly toast slices under a preheated grill.

Layer slices in a 23 x 30 x 4cm (9 x 12 x 1 3/4 in) ovenproof dish and scatter with blueberries.

Scrape seeds from vanilla pod into a small saucepan, add cream and vanilla pod and bring almost to the boil over moderate heat. In a bowl, lightly whisk eggs and sugar together, then whisk in hot cream. Remove vanilla pod. Slowly pour custard into dish, allowing panettone to soak up the liquid.

Place dish in a water bath and bake for 50 minutes or until custard is just set and top is golden. Remove from oven and serve warm or cool accompanied by crème fraîche.

This dessert would also make a great breakfast dish. You may like to try this pancake recipe adding about 250g (8 oz) of blueberries to the batter and serve with maple syrup. You must use cavendish bananas as lady finger bananas will toughen during cooking.

Buttermilk pancake with grilled banana, caramel and double cream

Serves 10

250g (9 oz) plain flour
pinch of salt
1 tablespoon baking powder
1 teaspoon bicarbonate of soda
100g (3½ oz) caster sugar
500ml (18 fl oz) buttermilk
4 eggs, separated
clarified butter (Basics page 164)
125g (4½ oz) unsalted butter
10 bananas (cavendish)
200g (7 oz) soft brown sugar
1 lemon, juice only
double cream

Combine flour, salt, baking powder, bicarbonate of soda and sugar in a large bowl and mix well. Make a well in the centre. Whisk buttermilk and egg yolks together then add to dry ingredients and stir to form a batter. Whisk egg whites to soft peaks and fold into mixture.

Preheat grill to moderately hot. Brush hot blini pans with clarified butter (or use a heavy-based frying pan) and cook batter over moderate heat until the underside is golden. Place blini pans under preheated grill to cook second side or if using a frypan gently turn pancakes, when bubbles burst, using a spatula.

Heat a heavy-based frying pan over moderately high heat and melt the butter. Slice bananas diagonally into three equal sections and add to pan. Sprinkle with brown sugar and cook briefly until sugar is caramelised, but bananas are not too soft. Adjust to taste with the lemon juice.

To serve, place a pancake on each plate, top with 3 pieces of caramelised banana and accompany with a spoonful of double cream to one side.

This recipe makes a substantial quantity but lavosh will keep well in an airtight container. Alternatively the dough freezes well. At e'cco I prefer to just feature one cheese usually accompanied with dried fruits, crisp apple, pear or quince jam, and always this lavosh. Some of my favourite cheeses are Gippsland Shadows of Blue, King Island Black Label Brie, Gorgonzola, Parmigiano, Taleggio, Woodside Edith Goat's Cheese, Pyengana Cheddar and, of course, Gabrielle Kervella's goat cheeses.

Cheese plate with fruit and lavosh

400g (13 oz) plain flour
1½ teaspoons sea salt
1 teaspoon sugar
2 tablespoons poppy seed
2 tablespoons sesame seed
1 egg, lightly beaten
200ml (7 fl oz) milk
50g (2 oz) unsalted butter, melted

In a large bowl, combine flour, salt, sugar and seeds. Make a well in the centre and pour in egg, milk and melted butter, then mix well to combine.

Remove dough from bowl and knead lightly on a floured surface. Wrap in plastic food wrap and refrigerate for one hour. (At this stage dough can be frozen).

Preheat oven to 180°C (350°F/Gas 4). Remove dough from refrigerator, unwrap and roll portions of the dough very thinly, about 2mm (1/16 in) thick (or roll dough through a pasta machine) Place on oven trays lined with baking (silicone) paper. Bake for 5-8 minutes or until dry and pale golden. Remove from oven and cool on wire racks. Store in an airtight container until ready to use.

Serve with a selection of cheese and fruit.

ice cream

Vanilla bean
White chocolate
Pistachio
Rum and raisin
Espresso
Coconut
Passionfruit
Burnt caramel
Chocolate malt
Pineapple sorbet

You can vary this ice cream in a number of ways by following the directions below.

Vanilla bean ice cream

Makes 1.25 litres (2 pt)

300g (10 oz) caster sugar

12 egg yolks
2 vanilla pods
500ml (18 fl oz) milk
500ml (18 fl oz) cream (see Glossary)

In a bowl, lightly whisk sugar and egg yolks together. Split vanilla pods lengthwise and scrape seeds from pods into a 2 litre (3½ pt) saucepan. Add vanilla pods to pan with the milk and cream and bring almost to the boil. Whisk hot milk mixture into eggs then return mixture to clean saucepan over moderate heat.

Using a wooden spoon, stir constantly until custard thickens and coats the back of the spoon. Do not let mixture boil. Strain through a fine sieve, then refrigerate until cold. Churn in an ice cream machine. Store in freezer.

For white chocolate ice cream: Prepare ice cream as directed. When fully churned, stir in 250g (9 oz) grated best quality white chocolate.

For pistachio ice cream: Blanch 180g (6 oz) shelled unsalted pistachios in boiling water, drain and rub in clean towel to remove most of the skin. Pulse briefly in a food processor to roughly chop. Mix in 60ml (2 fl oz) kirsch. Prepare ice cream as directed and when fully churned, stir through pistachio mixture.

For rum and raisin ice cream: Soak 150g (5 oz) raisins in 125ml (4½ fl oz) dark rum overnight. Prepare ice cream as directed, except omit vanilla. When fully churned, add rum and raisins.

For espresso ice cream: Prepare ice cream omitting vanilla. Add 100g (3½ oz) whole coffee beans and 60ml (2 fl oz) espresso coffee to milk and cream mixture. Do not strain coffee beans out until just prior to churning.

For coconut ice cream: Prepare ice cream, omitting vanilla. Substitute coconut cream for the milk and reduce caster sugar to 200g (7 oz). When half churned, add 4 tablespoons lightly roasted desiccated coconut and continue to churn.

For passionfruit: Prepare ice cream, except omit vanilla and milk and increase cream to 700ml (1¼ pt). Add 300 ml (11 fl oz) strained passionfruit to egg, sugar and hot cream mixture before returning to clean saucepan to finish cooking.

Burnt caramel ice cream

Makes 1.25 litres (2 pt)

300g (10 oz) caster sugar
125ml (4½ fl oz) water
12 egg yolks
500ml (18 fl oz) cream
500ml (18 fl oz) milk

Place 200g (7 oz) of the sugar and the water in a 2 litre (3½ pt) saucepan over moderate heat and stir to dissolve sugar. Bring to a boil and do not stir again. Boil until syrup becomes dark golden in colour, then immediately remove from heat. Taking care, as mixture will spit, gradually stir in cream and milk. Return pan to heat and bring mixture almost to the boil.

In a bowl, lightly whisk remaining sugar and egg yolks together. Whisk hot milk mixture into eggs, then return to clean saucepan over moderate heat.

Using a wooden spoon, stir constantly until custard thickens, taking care not to boil. Strain through a fine sieve and refrigerate until cold. Churn in an ice cream machine and store in freezer.

Chocolate malt ice cream

Makes 1.25 litres (2 pt)

50g (2 oz) caster sugar
8 egg yolks
500ml (18 fl oz) milk
230g (8 oz) best quality milk chocolate, chopped
65g (2¼ oz) malted milk powder
500ml (18 fl oz) cream

In a bowl, lightly whisk sugar and egg yolks together. In a 2 litre (3½ pt) saucepan, heat milk until almost boiling, remove from heat and whisk in chopped chocolate and malted milk powder. Allow chocolate to melt fully before whisking in cream to decrease temperature. Whisk hot milk mixture into eggs and return to clean saucepan over moderate heat.

Using a wooden spoon, stir constantly until custard thickens, taking care not to boil. Strain custard through a fine sieve and refrigerate until cold. Churn in an ice cream machine and store in freezer.

To prepare the pineapple juice, dice pineapple flesh from two fresh pineapples. Purèe in a food processor, then pass through a sieve before measuring the required quantity.

Pineapple sorbet

Makes 1.5 litres (3 pts)

500g (17 oz) caster sugar
500ml (18 fl oz) water
800ml (1 pt 8 oz) strained pineapple juice

Combine sugar and water in a saucepan over moderate heat, stirring to completely dissolve the sugar. Bring to the boil, then remove pan from heat and add pineapple juice. Refrigerate until cold. Churn in an ice cream machine and store in freezer.

basics

Clarified butter
Cooking chickpeas
Roasting peppers
Oven-roasted tomatoes
Soft poached eggs
Hommus
Pesto
Tapenade
Garlic confit
Roasted garlic mayonnaise
Chilli oil
Hollandaise
Salsa verde
Rich tomato sauce
Red wine vinaigrette
Balsamic dressing
Lemon dressing
Burnt orange vinaigrette
Red pepper essence
Salted lemons
Onion jam
Orange confit
Date and lime chutney
Apple and currant chutney
Shortcrust pastry – savoury
Shortcrust pastry – sweet
Jus
Stocks – beef/chicken/roasted chicken
Slow-cooked duck
Beurre blanc
Braised veal shanks or oxtail

Clarified butter

250g (9 oz) unsalted butter

To clarify place butter in a small saucepan over low heat, allow it to melt and separate. Carefully pour off melted butter, leaving milk solids behind. Discard milk solids and refrigerate clarified butter.

The main advantage of clarified butter is that it can be heated to a much higher temperature than butter before it burns.

Cooking chickpeas

You can also use this method to cook dried beans.

Cooking time is dependent on the age of the chickpeas or beans, but reasonably fresh dried chickpeas will cook in about 45 minutes; borlotti beans can take up to 1½ hours.

400g (13 oz-about 2 cups) dried chickpeas

2 teaspoons bicarbonate of soda

1 onion, halved, roots intact

1 bay leaf

few sprigs thyme

Pick over and wash chickpeas, then drain and place in a large bowl with bicarbonate of soda. Cover well with cold water and refrigerate overnight.

Next day, drain chickpeas, rinse, drain again and place in a large saucepan. Cover well with fresh cold water, add the onion, bay leaf, thyme and bring to the boil, skimming off any impurities that rise to the surface. Reduce heat and simmer until chickpeas are tender, skimming occasionally. Drain, discard flavourings and use as directed in recipes. Will keep 1-2 days, refrigerated.

Roasting peppers

Preheat oven to 250°C (500°F/Gas 9). Wash and dry peppers (capsicum) and rub well with olive oil. Season with salt/pepper. Place on an oven tray and roast until skin is well-blistered, turning once or twice. You can also roast peppers on a barbecue or under a hot grill.

Place peppers in a bowl, cover with plastic food wrap and allow to cool. When the skin has steamed away from the flesh, peel it off and discard with ribs and seeds. Use the roasted flesh as directed in recipes.

Oven-roasted tomatoes

Tomatoes can be prepared several days in advance and stored in a covered container in the refrigerator until required.

roma (italian plum) tomatoes, halved lengthwise
olive oil
salt/pepper
thyme leaves
balsamic vinegar (optional)
crushed garlic (optional)

Preheat oven to 180°C (350°F/Gas 4). Place tomato halves in a single layer on an oiled baking tray. Whisk desired flavourings into a little olive oil and brush liberally over tomatoes. Roast tomatoes for 15 minutes then reduce oven temperature to 120°C (250°F/Gas 1/2) and roast a further 1-1½ hours.

Soft poached eggs

2 litres (3½ pt) water
2 teaspoons white vinegar
eggs

Bring water to the boil in a large shallow pan, reduce heat and add the vinegar. Break eggs, one at a time, onto a saucer then slide egg from saucer into the gently simmering water. Cook no more than 3 or 4 eggs at a time. Eggs are cooked when the white is set but the yolk is still soft.

Using a slotted spoon, remove poached eggs from pan and drain on absorbent paper. To serve, gently lift eggs from paper and arrange on serving plate or use as directed in recipes.

Eggs can be poached up to 24 hours in advance, slipped into a bowl of iced water to cool. Cover the bowl and store in the refrigerator. Reheat eggs by carefully lifting them from the water and sliding them into a pot of gently simmering water. Allow 1 minute to heat through, remove and drain well on absorbent paper.

Hommus

Makes about 600g (21 oz)

500g (17 oz – about 2 cups) cooked chickpeas (Basics page 164)
½ lemon, juice only
1 tablespoon white wine vinegar
1 tablespoon tahini (sesame seed paste)
2 heads garlic confit (Basics page 167)
salt/pepper
½ cup (125ml/4½ fl oz) extra-virgin olive oil
¼ cup (60ml/2 fl oz) chickpea cooking liquor or water

Place chickpeas, lemon juice, vinegar, tahini, roasted garlic flesh, salt and black pepper to taste in a food processor and process briefly to combine. With machine running, drizzle in the olive oil. Adjust consistency by adding cooking liquor or water. Taste and adjust seasonings.

Pesto

Makes about 1½ cups (375ml/13 fl oz)

4 cups (about 120g/4 oz) basil leaves
3 cloves garlic, crushed
½ lemon, juice only
1 cup (250ml/9 fl oz) extra-virgin olive oil
½ cup (75g/2½ oz) pine nuts, roasted
50g (2 oz) parmesan, freshly grated
salt/pepper

Pick over basil leaves, wash and dry in a salad-spinner. Place basil in a food processor with the garlic and lemon juice, process until well combined. With machine running, drizzle in olive oil. Add pine nuts and parmesan and process briefly to retain some texture to the pesto. Season with salt and pepper to taste.

Store pesto with a thin layer of olive oil covering the surface in an airtight container. It will last several days in the refrigerator.

Tapenade

Makes about 1¼ cups (310 ml/11 fl oz)

250g (9 oz) pitted black olives
50g (2 oz) anchovy fillets in oil, drained
25g (about 1 oz) salted capers, well rinsed
2 cloves garlic, crushed
2 tablespoons extra-virgin olive oil

Combine olives, anchovies, capers and garlic in a food processor and process until well chopped. With machine running, drizzle in the oil. Store tapenade in a sealed container in the refrigerator.

Garlic confit

There are two methods for preparing garlic confit that will give a rich, sweet flavour to the garlic. One is to roast heads of garlic; the other is to simmer them in oil. Squeeze the flesh from the heads of garlic as you require it for recipes.

To roast garlic: Slow-roasted garlic is much more palatable than raw garlic. Preheat oven to 200°C (400°F/Gas 6). Cut off and discard the top one-third from 6 heads of garlic and place, root end down, in the centre of a square of aluminium foil. Drizzle cut tops liberally with extra-virgin olive oil, then wrap heads in foil to enclose completely. Place foil parcel on an oven tray and bake for 1 hour, or until garlic is soft. Cool. Garlic will keep for several days in the refrigerator.

To confit garlic: Cut off and discard the top one-third from 6 heads of garlic and place, root end down, in a saucepan. Cover heads with vegetable oil and cook over low heat for 45-60 minutes or until soft. The long slow cooking is required to develop flavour. Cool, then transfer garlic and oil to a storage container and refrigerate. Use the flesh and flavoured oil as needed in recipes.

Roasted garlic mayonnaise

Makes about 2 cups (500ml/18 fl oz)

2 egg yolks
2 teaspoons dijon mustard
2 tablespoons white wine vinegar
½ lemon, juice only
salt/pepper
1 cup (250ml/9 fl oz) extra-virgin olive oil
1 cup (250ml/9 fl oz) vegetable oil
2 heads garlic confit (Basics this page)

Place egg yolks, mustard, vinegar, lemon juice and seasonings in a blender and blend briefly. Combine oils and, with machine running, slowly drizzle in until the mayonnaise becomes well-blended and thick. Squeeze the flesh from the roasted garlic into the mayonnaise and combine. You may need to thin the mayonnaise with a little hot water. Taste for acidity and seasonings and adjust with lemon juice, salt and pepper.

Chilli oil

Makes about 220ml (7½ fl oz)

4 red chillies, seeded and finely diced
2 cloves garlic, crushed
salt/pepper
2 lemons, juice only
½ cup (125ml/4 fl oz) extra-virgin olive oil

Place chillies, garlic, seasonings and lemon juice in a bowl and gradually whisk in the olive oil until well blended. Allow to infuse several hours.

Hollandaise

Makes about 300ml (10 fl oz)

½ teaspoon white peppercorns
1 bay leaf
1 sprig thyme
1 shallot (french shallot)
¼ cup (60ml/2 fl oz) white wine vinegar
¼ cup (60ml/2 fl oz) white wine
3 egg yolks
1 cup (250ml/9 fl oz) clarified butter, very hot (Basics page 164)
½ lemon, juice only
pinch cayenne pepper
sea salt

Place peppercorns, bay leaf, thyme, shallot, vinegar and wine in a small saucepan. Bring to the boil and boil until liquid is reduced to two-thirds original volume. Strain.

Place egg yolks in a blender and, with machine running, add 1 tablespoon of the very hot reduction, then slowly drizzle in clarified butter. Flavour with lemon juice, cayenne and salt to taste. Hollandaise can be thinned with a little boiling water, if needed. Keep in a warm place, and use as soon as possible as this sauce cannot be reheated. (Refrigerate balance of reduction for future use. It will keep several weeks.)

Salsa verde

Makes 1 cup (250ml/9 fl oz)

1 cup basil leaves
1 cup flat-leaf parsley
2 cloves garlic, crushed
50g (2 oz) salted capers, well rinsed
3 anchovy fillets in oil, drained, rinsed and dried
1 tablespoon red wine vinegar (see Glossary)
2½ tablespoons extra-virgin olive oil
2 teaspoons dijon mustard
salt/pepper

Finely chop the herbs, garlic, capers and anchovies and place in a bowl. Whisking well, drizzle in the vinegar, then the oil. Flavour with mustard, salt and black pepper. Store, covered, in the refrigerator.

MANGOES

Rich tomato sauce

Makes about 600ml (21 fl oz)

For some applications you may need to thin this sauce with a little chicken stock.

2 tablespoons olive oil
3 shallots (french shallots), sliced
4 cloves garlic, finely chopped
2 x 400g (13 oz) cans roma (italian plum) tomatoes, puréed
6 roma (italian plum) tomatoes, skinned and chopped
2 tablespoons herbs such as oregano and thyme, chopped
salt/pepper
pinch of sugar, optional

Heat oil in a heavy-based pan over moderate heat and sauté shallots and garlic until shallots are transparent. Add canned and fresh tomatoes and herbs. Reduce heat and simmer for 45 minutes or until tomatoes are well-reduced, taking care sauce does not burn. Season with salt and black pepper. If sauce tastes too acidic, add a pinch of sugar.

Red wine vinaigrette

Makes about 400ml (14 fl oz)

2 cloves garlic, crushed
1/2 lemon, juice only
100ml (3 1/2 fl oz) red wine vinegar (see Glossary)
300ml (11 fl oz) extra-virgin olive oil
salt/pepper

Combine garlic, lemon juice and vinegar in a bowl. Whisk in olive oil, then season with salt and black pepper to taste.

Balsamic dressing

Makes 200ml (7 fl oz)

1/4 cup (60ml/2 fl oz) best quality balsamic vinegar
1 clove garlic, crushed
pinch of sugar
salt/pepper
180ml (6 fl oz) extra-virgin olive oil

Place vinegar, garlic, sugar and seasoning in a bowl and gradually whisk in the olive oil until well blended.

Lemon dressing

Makes about 400ml (14 fl oz)

I recommend Hill Farm Mountain Pepper mustard from Tasmania for this dressing, but if unavailable, any good-quality grain mustard can be used.

100ml (3½ oz) lemon juice
2 teaspoons grain mustard
1 tablespoon thyme leaves
150ml (5 fl oz) vegetable oil
150ml (5 fl oz) extra-virgin olive oil
salt/pepper

Place lemon juice, mustard and thyme in bowl, whisk in combined oils, then season to taste with salt and black pepper.

Burnt orange vinaigrette

Makes about 1 cup (250ml/9 fl oz)

600ml (21 fl oz) orange juice, freshly squeezed
2½ tablespoons extra-virgin olive oil
salt/pepper

Boil the orange juice in a heavy-based saucepan until reduced to 200ml (7 fl oz), then remove from heat and cool slightly before whisking in the olive oil. Season to taste with salt and black pepper.

Red pepper essence

Makes about 1 cup (250ml/9 fl oz)

This sauce goes well with all seafood, grilled polenta and gnocchi.

2 tablespoons olive oil
4 red peppers (capsicum), seeded and chopped
4 shallots (french shallots), thinly sliced
¼ cup basil leaves
1 star anise
3 cloves garlic, unpeeled and lightly crushed
30ml (1 fl oz) white wine vinegar
200ml (7 fl oz) dry vermouth (preferably Noilly Prat)
600ml (21 fl oz) chicken stock (Basics page 176)
100ml (3½ fl oz) orange juice, freshly squeezed
salt/pepper

Heat olive oil in a heavy-based saucepan over moderate heat. Add red peppers, shallots, basil, star anise and whole garlic cloves and gently sweat for 5 minutes or until shallots are softened but not coloured.

Add vinegar to pan and cook for 2 minutes. Add vermouth, cook 2 minutes more, then add stock and bring to the boil. Boil until liquid reduces by half.

Remove garlic and star anise, then purée mixture in a blender, adding orange juice. Strain sauce and set aside until required.

Salted lemons

Diced salted lemon is used to enhance seafood dishes, couscous or moroccan-style foods. The skin of traditionally preserved lemons need to be well washed before use as they are much saltier than lemons salted using this method.

4 lemons
125g (4½ oz) maldon sea salt
750ml (1¼ pt) water, approximately

Choose a saucepan that will fit the lemons snugly. Place lemons in pan with salt and enough water to cover them. Invert a small plate over lemons to keep them submerged.

Bring to the boil, then reduce heat and simmer for 20 minutes or until the skins are soft. Drain lemons and cool then store in a covered container in the refrigerator until needed. They'll keep up to two weeks. To use, scrape out and discard the flesh and dice the skin finely.

Onion jam

Makes about 2 cups (500ml/18 fl oz)

10 red onions, peeled
1 tablespoon olive oil
1 tablespoon unsalted butter
100ml (3½ fl oz) red wine vinegar (see Glossary)
salt/pepper

Halve onions and remove ends. Place flat on a board and cut into thin semi-circles. Heat oil and butter in a wide, shallow heavy-based pan over moderate heat. Add the onions and allow to sweat for 10 minutes. Add vinegar and cook for 15-20 minutes or until onions are dark in colour and jam-like in consistency. Season with salt and black pepper. Cool, then store in a covered container in the refrigerator.

Orange confit

1 cup (250g/9 oz) caster sugar
1 cup (250ml/9 fl oz) water
1 star anise
1 cinnamon quill
3 whole cloves
½ cup (125ml/4 fl oz) orange juice, freshly squeezed
3 oranges, skin and pith removed, thickly sliced

Place sugar, water and spices in a heavy-based pan over moderate heat and cook until mixture is quite a dark caramel, taking care not to let it burn. Remove pan from heat and add orange juice carefully – toffee mixture will spit! Return pan to heat and stir until mixture is smooth.

Preheat oven to 160°C (325°F/Gas 3). Place orange slices in an ovenproof dish, pour syrup mixture over and cover with aluminium foil. Bake for 20 minutes or until oranges are soft. Allow oranges to cool in syrup.

Date and lime chutney

Makes about 1 litre (1 3/4 pt)

- 2 tablespoons olive oil
- 1/4 cup (about 30g/1 oz) red chillies, thinly sliced
- 1/4 cup (30g/1 oz) fresh ginger, peeled and thinly sliced
- 2 cloves garlic, crushed
- 1 red onion, diced
- 1 tablespoon cumin seed, roasted and ground
- pinch dried chilli flakes
- 5 limes
- 1.25kg (2lb 12 oz) fresh dates, pitted
- 1 1/2 cups (375ml/13 fl oz) water
- 1/2 cup (125ml/4 1/2 fl oz) white wine vinegar
- 1 1/2 tablespoons brown sugar
- 1/2 cup coriander leaves

Heat the oil in a large, heavy-based saucepan over moderate heat. Add chillies, ginger and garlic, sweat until soft. Add the onion, ground cumin and chilli flakes, cook until onion is soft.

Grate the zest from 3 of the limes. Remove all peel and pith from the 5 limes, then roughly dice flesh. Add to pan with the dates, water, vinegar and brown sugar. Simmer, stirring occasionally, for 40 minutes or until mixture becomes tacky. Allow mixture to cool, then fold in fresh coriander. Bottle chutney in sterilised jars, seal and store in the refrigerator.

Apple and currant chutney

Makes about 1 1/2 cups (375g/13 oz)

- 4 granny smith apples, peeled, cored and diced
- 1/2 cup (75g/2 1/2 oz) currants
- 2 cloves garlic, chopped
- 1/2 cup (90g/3 oz) brown sugar
- 90ml (3 fl oz) cider vinegar
- 1 tablespoon marjoram leaves
- 1 cup (250ml/9 fl oz) water
- sea salt

Combine all ingredients in a heavy-based saucepan over moderate heat and bring to the boil. Reduce heat to low and gently simmer, stirring frequently, until thick and glossy. Taste and adjust seasoning, if required. Store, covered, in the refrigerator.

Shortcrust pastry – savoury

- 300g (11 oz) plain flour
- 155g (5 1/2 oz) unsalted butter
- pinch sea salt
- 1 tablespoon, approximately, very cold water

Combine the flour, butter and salt in a food processor and process until mixture resembles breadcrumbs. Process, adding just enough water to bring pastry together on the blade, do not overwork. Knead lightly, wrap in plastic food wrap and refrigerate for 1 hour before using.

Shortcrust pastry – sweet

350g (12 oz) unsalted butter
155g (5½ oz/1¼ cups) icing sugar
4 egg yolks
500g (17 oz/4 cups) plain flour, sifted
2½ tablespoons, approximately, very cold water

In a food processor, cream the butter and sugar together. Add the egg yolks, one at a time, mixing well after each addition. Mix in flour, then add just enough water to bring pastry together on the blade, do not overwork. Knead lightly, wrap in plastic food wrap and refrigerate for 1 hour before using.

To blind bake a pastry tart shell

1 egg, beaten lightly, for egg wash

Preheat oven to 180°C (350°F/Gas 4). Roll out rested pastry 3mm (⅛ in) thick and gently ease into tart tin. Rest a further 30 minutes in the refrigerator or freezer.

Line pastry shell with a piece of baking (silicone) paper – or use parchment or foil, fill with pastry weights such as raw rice or split peas and bake for 20 minutes. Remove weights and paper and brush egg wash over shell. Reduce oven temperature to160°C (325°F/Gas 3) and bake a further 10 minutes, or until golden.

Jus

Jus is simply reduced stock or an unthickened meat sauce. Good delicatessens and some restaurants sell jus for the cook's convenience, but otherwise, you can prepare your own, as follows.

Bring four litres (7 pt) beef stock to the boil over moderate heat. Continue to boil until stock is reduced by two-thirds, occasionally skimming the surface of impurities. The resulting sauce should be thick and glossy.

If, after obtaining the required flavour, the jus is still not of coating consistency, it can be lightly thickened with arrowroot, as follows: Combine 1 tablespoon arrowroot with ¼ cup (60ml/2 fl oz) cold water, then gradually drizzle just enough into the boiling stock, whisking constantly until the sauce coats the back of a spoon. Strain while hot, cool, then store in small containers in the refrigerator or freezer.

Stocks can be reduced to concentrate flavour and reduce the bulk for easier storage. Many good delicatessens and some restaurants will sell reduced stock and/or jus (Basics page 175) for domestic use. Otherwise, you can prepare your own from these recipes.

Stocks

Beef stock

Makes about 4 litres (7 pt)

2.5kg (5½ lb) beef neck bones
2.5kg (5½ lb) oxtail, cut
2 tablespoons olive oil
2 onions, diced
2 carrots, diced
2 sticks celery, diced
2 leeks, sliced and washed
½ head garlic, halved horizontally
90g (3 oz) field (open-flat or swiss brown) mushrooms, wiped and sliced
½ cup (125g/4½ oz) italian tomato paste (concentrated purée)
2 cups (500ml/18 fl oz) red wine
1 pig's trotter
1 teaspoon white peppercorns
3 bay leaves
6 sprigs thyme
few parsley stalks

Preheat oven to 220° (425°F/Gas 7). Place bones and oxtail in a large roasting pan and roast until well browned. Drain off the rendered fat.

Heat olive oil in a large stockpot over high heat, add onions, carrots, celery, leeks, garlic, mushrooms and sauté until well-coloured. Add tomato paste and cook, stirring, for 2 minutes. Add wine and simmer until liquid reduces by half.

Add roasted bones to vegetables with the pig's trotter, peppercorns and herbs and cover well with cold water. Bring to the boil, skimming off any impurities that rise to the surface, then reduce heat and gently simmer for 8 hours. The stock pot may need topping up with water to keep bones submerged. Continue to skim occasionally to remove impurities that will rise to the surface of the pot. Strain stock and refrigerate or freeze until ready to use.

Chicken stock

Makes about 3 litres (5 pt)

2kg (4 lb 6 oz) chicken bones and carcasses
1 carrot, diced
1 onion, diced
1 leek, sliced and washed
1 stick celery, diced
3 cloves garlic, unpeeled, lightly crushed
1 teaspoon white peppercorns
2 bay leaves
4 sprigs thyme
few parsley stalks

Rinse chicken bones in cold water and place in a large stockpot with all remaining ingredients. Cover well with cold water and bring to the boil, skimming off any impurities that rise to the surface. Reduce heat and simmer for 1½-2 hours or until a good flavour develops. Continue to skim occasionally. Strain stock and refrigerate or freeze until ready to use.

Roasted chicken stock

Makes about 3 litres (5 pt)

2kg (4 lb) chicken bones and carcasses
1 carrot, diced
1 onion, diced
I leek, sliced and washed
3 cloves garlic, unpeeled, lightly crushed
4 sprigs thyme
1 bay leaf
1 teaspoon white peppercorns, crushed
few parsley stalks
1 cup (250ml/8 fl oz) white wine

Preheat oven to 200°C (400°F/Gas 6). Place chicken carcasses in a roasting pan and roast until golden. Take care not to colour chicken too much as this will make the stock bitter.

Using tongs or slotted spoon, transfer bones to a large stockpot and add remaining ingredients, except the wine. Cover with cold water and bring to the boil, skimming off any impurities that rise to the surface.

Pour off and discard fat from roasting pan then place pan over moderate heat and deglaze by adding the wine and stirring well to loosen the sediment. Pour mixture into stockpot and continue to simmer gently for 1½ hours, skimming occasionally. Strain stock, cool and refrigerate or freeze until ready to use.

Slow-cooked duck

Serves 4

It is possible to confit duck legs in light olive oil if duck or goose fat is either difficult to find or you would prefer not to use it. Make sure you use light olive oil, rather than extra-virgin, as its flavour would be overwhelming. However, you cannot achieve the same depth of flavour without using fat.

This duck can be cooked up to 1 week in advance and stored in the refrigerator.

Maryland portions are the thigh-and-leg as one piece, with skin on.

4 duck maryland (thigh-and-leg) portions from 2.2kg (4½ lb) ducks
2 sprigs thyme
I lemon, zest removed in strips
I orange, zest removed in strips
6 cloves garlic, unpeeled and lightly crushed
3 star anise
salt
500ml (18 fl oz) duck or goose fat or light olive oil, enough to cover legs

Prepare duck portions by removing each thigh bone, then running a sharp knife around the bone just below the knuckle end of each leg – this allows the meat to shrink down during cooking. Place portions in a shallow dish and sprinkle with thyme, lemon and orange zest, garlic, star anise and a generous amount of salt. Rub mixture well over portions, then cover and refrigerate for 24 hours.

Preheat oven to 150°C (300°F/Gas 2). Heat fat or oil in saucepan until quite hot, pour over duck then place dish in oven and slow-cook for 2-3 hours or until tender. Cool, then store duck in a clean container covered with the cooking fat to seal and preserve it. Refrigerate container.

To serve, preheat oven to 180°C (350°F/Gas 4). Remove duck from fat and place in oven until warm, then place under a preheated hot grill just prior to serving to crisp the skin.

Beurre blanc

Makes about 350ml (12 fl oz)

$^{1}/_{2}$ cup (125ml/4 fl oz) white wine vinegar
$^{1}/_{2}$ cup (125ml/4 fl oz) white wine
2 shallots (french shallots), thinly sliced
3 white peppercorns
1 bay leaf
1 cup (250ml/8 fl oz) cream
250g (8 oz) cold unsalted butter, cubed
$^{1}/_{2}$ lemon, juice only
sea salt and freshly ground white pepper

Combine vinegar, wine, shallots, peppercorns and bay leaf in a small saucepan over moderate heat. Bring to the boil and cook until liquid reduces by two-thirds. Strain reduction into a clean saucepan and return to heat.

Whisk in cream and return sauce to the boil. Reduce mixture by one-third. Briskly whisk in the butter, piece by piece – sauce should appear thick and glossy. Season with lemon juice, salt and white pepper to taste. Keep warm until required.

Braised veal shanks or oxtail

plain flour, for dusting
salt/pepper
8 veal shanks or 2kg (4 lb 6 oz) cut oxtail
1 onion
1 carrot
1 stick celery
1 leek, halved lengthwise and washed
$^{1}/_{2}$ cup (125ml/4$^{1}/_{2}$ fl oz) olive oil
5 cloves garlic, unpeeled, lightly crushed
few sprigs rosemary
few sprigs thyme
3 tablespoons italian tomato paste (concentrated purée)
400ml (14 fl oz) red wine
1-2 litres (1$^{3}/_{4}$-3$^{1}/_{2}$ pt) beef stock (Basics page 176)

Preheat oven to 160°C (325°F/Gas 3). Season flour with salt and pepper and lightly coat shanks or oxtails, shaking to remove the excess. Peel and dice onion, carrot, celery and leek into 1cm ($^{1}/_{2}$ in) pieces.

Heat olive oil in a heavy-based frying pan and seal the shanks or oxtails well, transferring them to a large flameproof casserole as they brown. Add the diced vegetables with the garlic and herbs to pan and cook until golden. Add tomato paste and cook 5 minutes. Spoon mixture over meat in casserole.

Deglaze pan with wine, stirring to loosen the sediment, and pour mixture into casserole. Add enough stock to casserole to cover contents and bring to the boil. Cover casserole with lid or foil and bake 1-1$^{1}/_{2}$ hours (for shanks); 2-2$^{1}/_{2}$ hours (for oxtails) or until meat is tender and pulls away from the bones. Remove from oven and allow to cool in the stock.

Carefully remove all meat from bones, discarding any fat or sinews. Strain the stock, discarding vegetables, and place in a heavy-based saucepan. Boil uncovered, over high heat until reduced to a rich, glossy sauce. Store meat and reduced sauce in separate containers in the refrigerator until needed.

Notes for the cook

Equipment

The heavy-based pans referred to throughout this book are sauté pans of heavy gauge mild steel, 22 or 24cm (8 or 9½ in) in diameter, and about 4cm (1¾ in) deep. They are designed to be used both over high flame and in hot ovens. A good brand to look for is Matfer from France. After use, scrub with hot water (no detergent), dry over heat and rub with oil to avoid oxidation.

Using a sauté pan over direct heat, then immediately transferring it to a hot oven is my preferred method of cooking meat. This avoids heat loss and consequently stops the food stewing. These pans are inexpensive and, once you have used this method of cooking meats, you will also be convinced.

However I have described a method of using a domestic frying pan and transferring the food to a hot oven tray if a sauté pan is unavailable.

Our stainless steel cake rings are 24cm (9½ in) in diameter and 4cm (1¾ in) high and have no base. A lined springform tin may be substituted for a cake ring although I have yet to find one with low enough sides to suit our tarts.

Standard measures and conversions

1 cup	250 ml (8 fl oz)
1 Australian tablespoon (4 teaspoons)	20 ml
1 UK tablespoon (3 teaspoons)	15 ml
1 teaspoon	5 ml
1 ounce	28.4 grams
1 fluid ounce	28.4 ml

Ingredients

checking and adjusting seasonings – refers to tasting a dish and deciding whether or not it requires further flavouring generally with salt or pepper, but could also refer to checking for sweetness or acidity in dressings.

cream – means unthickened cream with at least 35% butterfat, double cream means unthickened cream with at least 45% butterfat.

egg size – 55-60g free-range are preferred.

herbs – all our recipes use fresh herbs. Prepare by removing wilted or damaged leaves. Wash and spin dry in a salad spinner.

salt/pepper – always means good quality sea salt flakes such as Maldon or Fleur de Sel (fine), and freshly cracked or ground black pepper.

salad leaves – Always wash salad leaves in copious amounts of cold water allowing any grit to fall to the bottom. Pick out old, damaged or tough sections/stalks. Place remaining leaves in a salad spinner or clean towel to dry. Dress dry salad leaves in a large kitchen bowl just before serving. This ensures an even coating of dressing.

spices – we always use whole spices and roast and grind them as required. All spices should be purchased and stored whole and separately roasted in a dry frying pan until fragrant. Grind to a powder using a mortar and pestle or coffee grinder.

Desserts and Ice creams

To alleviate discrepancies we have used weights and liquid measures in these recipes as they are more accurate than cup measurements.

Glossary

al dente – an Italian term literally translated as 'firm to the bite', used for pasta and risotto, meaning cooked until barely tender, retaining some resistance in the centre.

bain marie – see water bath

baker's flour – flour with high gluten content. If unavailable, substitute plain flour adding 10 per cent by weight of gluten flour (available from health food stores).

baking (silicone) paper – paper impregnated with silicone to give non-stick surfaces. Widely available at supermarkets.

baking powder – a raising agent consisting of bicarbonate of soda and cream of tartar mixed with a little flour.

balsamic vinegar – a northern Italian specialty vinegar originally from Modena. Vinegar is aged over many years, using a solera system where it darkens and becomes sweet and syrupy. Good balsamic is expensive. Beware of imitation balsamic where caramel is added to a lesser vinegar to enrich it.

bicarbonate of soda – a raising agent which improves the action of baking powder.

blanch – to immerse in boiling, often salted, water for a short period. This action par-cooks and stabilises colour. After blanching, refresh in iced water and drain.

blini pans – small 12cm (5 in) diameter x 2cm (3/4 in) high heavy gauge, mild steel pans used for cooking blini, rösti or pancakes. Matfer from France is a good brand to buy. Alternatively, use greased egg rings of similar diameter in a greased heavy-based frying pan.

brioche – a soft, sweet leavened bread enriched with eggs.

burghul – cracked whole wheat, also known as bulgar.

buttermilk – lightly acidic liquid left after churning butter. It is often used to lighten batters, cakes.

capers – green, unopened flower buds from a Mediterranean shrub. At e'cco we prefer salted capers but ensure they are well rinsed before using.

char-grilling – cooking over open flame or in a ridged grill pan.

ciabatta – crusty, flat, rectangular loaf of coarse textured northern Italian bread. Ciabatta literally means slipper.

chillies – the heat of chillies varies greatly with variety and growing conditions. Discarding seeds and membrane will lessen the heat. It is best to taste test raw chillies before using to establish the heat rating.

chorizo – spicy Spanish sausage available fresh or dried. At e'cco we mainly use the fresh variety.

coppa – Italian-style cured, boned, rolled shoulder of pork. If unavailable, use prosciutto.

cornflour (cornstarch) – always buy 100 per cent maize flour (not wheaten cornflour).

cornichons – small gherkins, without artificial colouring.

couverture – good quality chocolate with a high proportion of cocoa butter. It should melt easily on the tongue and not leave a fatty residue on the roof of the mouth. Dark/bitter chocolate has the highest percentage of cocoa butter and lowest percentage of sugar. We recommend and use Valrhona or Callebaut. Avoid compound cooking chocolate.

cream – as in creaming butter and sugar, is the technique of whisking together to dissolve sugar crystals. The mixture will become pale in colour and aerated.

crème fraîche – a distinctly sharp, semi-sour cream. Can be substituted with sour cream.

dariole mould – round, flat-bottomed, metal cup with flared sides, 125ml (4 fl oz) capacity.

deglaze – the action of adding stock, wine or water to a hot pan after browning ingredients. This incorporates any solids remaining in the pan into the liquid which is then added to the dish, giving added flavour.

devein – to remove intestinal tract from prawns, firstly remove the shell. Using a saté stick or skewer, insert it under the intestinal tract and gently lift to remove.

dice – means to chop into small, even cubes.

double boiler (double saucepan) – a method of gentle cooking by indirect heat obtained by sitting a tight-fitting saucepan or heatproof bowl over another pan quarter-filled with gently simmering water.

duck fat – available canned from delicatessens and gourmet food stores.

du Puy lentils – small, green lentils from France. Lentils are generally cooked without soaking first.

fold – to gently incorporate ingredients with a lifting and cutting action to avoid loss of aeration.

gelatine – half a teaspoon of gelatine powder equals one gelatine leaf. Leaf gelatine is considered superior to powder as it will set clear rather than cloudy.

goat's cheese – freshly made goat's cheese (goat ricotta or curd) in its simplest form, is mild and soft. As it ages and loses moisture if becomes stronger in flavour and more densely textured. Goat's cheese can be aged coated in ash, vine leaves, straw or it can form its own rind. These different outer layers will influence the flavour.

granny smith apple – firm, juicy, tart green-skinned cooking apple.

icing sugar (confectioner's sugar) – powdered pure version of white granulated sugar. Icing mixture has added cornflour to prevent lumps.

julienne – to cut into matchstick-sized strips.

jus – unthickened sauce or gravy, reduced from stock.

kaffir lime leaf – whole leaf added to dishes for its lime flavour, available fresh or frozen. Mainly used in southeast Asian cookery, especially Thai.

kiev cut – signifies chicken breast with wing, skin on, bone cleaned.

lardon – cut into rectangles 1 x 2cm (1/2 x 3/4 in). Often refers to pork fat.

lemon oil – lemon-infused olive oil. Commercially available brands are Colonna or Rex, both from Italy.

ligurian olives – small, mild tasting brownish/black olives from north western Italy. A good eating olive, also used for making olive oil.

mandoline – stainless steel manual slicing utensil.

mascarpone – sweet, rich cream (70-75% butterfat), usually made from cow's milk.

medallion – small round flat piece of food, usually meat.

mouli – a mill used to purée fruit, soup or vegetables.

mustard fruits – Italian glacé fruits packed in spicy mustard syrup.

olive oil – 'extra-virgin' refers to first quality olive oil with low acidity. Flavour varies regionally and between olive varieties from golden coloured, very mild oils to peppery, dark green. Price is a good guide to quality but choose a flavour you enjoy. Use sparingly in dressings, over breads and where the flavour of the oil is paramount. When not marked 'extra-virgin', olive oil is from a subsequent or heavier pressing of the olives. This type of oil is used for cooking and frying. It is generally a lot less expensive than extra-virgin olive oil.

palm sugar – Asian style sugar produced from palm sap, available as dark brown or light golden in colour. We prefer to use light palm sugar.

panettone – an airy, cylindrical-shaped yeasted bread originating in Milan, Italy. This egg enriched, fruit studded bread is used for Christmas celebrations and will keep for long periods.

parmesan – best quality is Parmigiano Reggiano from the Emilia-Romagna region of Italy. Genuine wheels have Parmigiano Reggiano stamped on the rind. This high quality parmesan is mainly used for garnishing and eating. A lesser quality grana padano or hard-grating cheese is generally used for cooking.

peanut oil – ground nut oil

pepitas – dried pumpkin seed

pickled ginger – generally thinly sliced ginger, pickled in brine or rice vinegar, pinkish in colour. Available at most supermarkets and Asian food stores.

pin boning – to remove bones from salmon fillet with tweezers or pliers.

poach – gentle method of cooking in barely simmering liquid.

prosciutto – salted, air-dried Italian style ham, always sliced paper thin.

purée – to pass through mouli or sieve, so no solids remain.

refresh – to quickly chill vegetables or salad leaves by plunging into iced water.

risotto rice – Arborio, Carnaroli or Vialone Nano are all excellent Italian risotto rice varieties. We prefer Vialone Nano. Risotto rice has the ability to cook to a creamy consistency with the grains remaining separate with a firm centre.

roasting nuts – nuts are best roasted by placing in a cake tin in a 180°C (350°F/Gas 4) oven until golden. Different varieties roast at different times.

roasting or grilling bacon, pancetta, prosciutto – Preheat oven to 190°C (375°F/Gas 5). Lay sliced meat in a single layer on greased or baking (silicone) paper-lined oven tray and roast in oven until crisp. Meat may also be grilled until crisp.

ruby chard – young red stemmed variety of silverbeet, also known as rainbow chard or red swiss chard.

salad spinner – utensil for drying salad leaves and herbs. Place washed leaves into inner basket then spin to expel water into outer container.

sambal oelek – Indonesian salted chilli paste.

sauté – to toss in small amount of fat (butter or oil) over high heat.

seal – to quickly cook food (usually meat) on both sides over very high heat, to seal in juices.

sear – to very quickly cook over fierce heat.

shallot (french shallot) – also known as eschalot or golden shallot. Small, elongated golden brown/pink-skinned onions which grow in tightly formed clusters like garlic. They have a fine, delicate slightly sweet and nutty flavour.

sherry vinegar – an intense, slightly fruity Spanish wine vinegar.

simmer – heated to just below boiling point where the surface of liquid should ripple but the bubbles should not break the surface.

sourdough – a chewy bread made using a fermented starter giving its characteristic sour taste. Sourness varies depending on recipe used.

springform tin – a circular metal cake pan with removable base that is held together by an expanding clamp on the side. Available in various diameters generally 6cm (2½ in) high.

stab/stick blender – electric handheld blender with central shaft which takes various attachments. Used for chopping, blending and whisking. Particularly good for puréeing soups directly in saucepans.

star anise – aniseed flavoured, eight-pointed pod of an evergreen Asian tree. Buy whole then roast and grind as required.

sweat – to cook gently over moderate heat, no colour should be developed.

tahini – Middle Eastern sesame seed paste, refrigerate after opening or it will oxidise.

taleggio – northern Italian soft, pungent cheese with a mild flavour.

terrine – 1.2 litre (2 pt) capacity, 25 x 7cm (10 x 2¾ in) lidded dish, generally of cast iron, we recommend Le Creuset.

thai fish sauce – also known as nam pla. Used as it has a more complex flavour than salt, we prefer brands such as Squid Brand or Three Crabs.

tomato paste (concentrated purée) – good quality Italian brands offer better flavour than supermarket varieties.

truffle oil – extra-virgin olive oil infused with the flavour of truffles. We prefer Terrabianca brand.

vanilla essence – always use good (Bourbon) quality vanilla essence, not imitation essence. Whole pods should be preferably Grade A1 from Madagascar, pliable and coated in vanillan crystals.

vinegars – always buy good quality vinegars. The wine vinegars used at e'cco are the Spanish brand, Forum, varietal vinegars. Both their Chardonnay (white) and Cabernet Sauvignon (red) are excellent.

water bath (bain marie) – a method of baking delicate foods using a cloth-lined dish filled with enough hot water to come halfway up the sides of the vessel containing the food.

wine – never cook with wine that you wouldn't consider drinking.

zest/zesting – outer layer of citrus fruit, without any white flesh (pith). Most often used finely grated. Utensil for removing zest is know as zester or use stiff-bladed vegetable peeler.

Index

*PAGE NUMBERS IN **BOLD** REFER TO PHOTOGRAPHS.*